INTRINSIC INCLUSION

Also by
Janet B. Reid, Ph.D. and Vincent R. Brown

Diversity Councils That Work

The Phoenix Principles:
Leveraging Inclusion to Transform Your Company

The Phoenix Principles:
A Comprehensive Guide to Transforming
Your Company through Inclusion

INTRINSIC INCLUSION

REBOOTING YOUR BIASED BRAIN

Janet B. Reid, Ph.D.
Vincent R. Brown

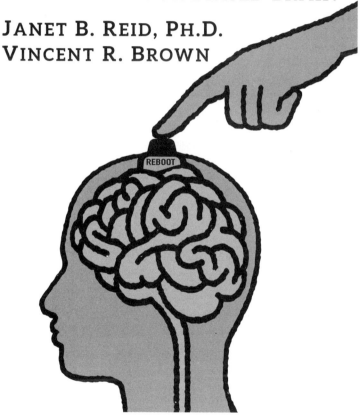

Foreword by John Pepper
Former CEO and Chairman, Procter & Gamble, and
Former Chairman of the board, Walt Disney Company

NEW PHOENIX PUBLISHING, LLC | CINCINNATI, OH

Published by
New Phoenix Publishing, LLC | Cincinnati, OH

Publisher's Cataloging-in-Publication Data
Reid, Janet B.

Intrinsic inclusion : rebooting your biased brain / Janet B. Reid and Vincent R. Brown. – Cincinnati, OH : New Phoenix Pub., LLC, 2021.

p. ; cm.

ISBN13: 978-0-9601023-0-3

1. Diversity in the workplace. 2. Equity. 3. Social integration. 4. Organizational behavior. 5. Corporate culture. 6. Intercultural communication. I. Title. II. Brown, Vincent R.

HF5549.5.M5 R45 2021
658.3008—dc23   2020906373

FIRST EDITION

Project coordination by Jenkins Group, Inc.
www.jenkinsgroupinc.com

Front cover illustration by Eric Tufford
Interior layout by Yvonne Fetig Roehler

Printed in the United States of America
25   24   23   22   21   •   5   4   3   2   1

Samuel E. Lynch
1952-2020

Your life was an exemplar of intrinsic inclusion.
We will miss you forever.

CONTENTS

FOREWORD

by JOHN PEPPER

Former CEO and Chairman, Procter & Gamble, and
Former Chairman of the Board, Walt Disney Company

When I joined P&G in 1963, its 35,000 or so employees were mostly white and male, and more than 90 percent were U.S. nationals. Today, its more than 100,000 employees include women and men representing virtually every nation, region, race, and ethnic background. The breadth of backgrounds and experience these employees bring to the job is a source of incalculable strength.

I've often been asked, "What is the single, most positive change you've seen in Procter & Gamble over the course of your career?" My answer: "The dramatically increased diversity of our employees." Yet, with all the progress that has been made, we are still not where we should be. And that's why *Intrinsic Inclusion: Rebooting Your Biased Brain* by Janet B. Reid, Ph.D. and Vincent R. Brown is so important.

My journey to appreciate the power of diversity, equity, and inclusion—and the challenge of achieving it—has been a long one, and it continues. Growing up, I wouldn't have understood what "diversity, equity, and inclusion" were all about. I grew up in a basically all-white city. When I went to Yale, it was all-male; only four of my thousand classmates were African Americans.

At P&G, I learned that we were only hiring men into Marketing Management. I didn't even notice that. It was the way things were. I had a hand in hiring the first woman directly into Marketing a few years after joining the company.

The journey to realize the value of diversity to the business didn't begin in the United States; it began in 1974, eleven years after I joined the company, serving as General Manager of P&G's Italian business. For the first time, I was living and working with people who spoke different languages and had different ethnic and cultural histories and substantially different life experiences from my own. It was this experience of being a cultural outsider that gradually opened my eyes to the power of diversity.

At first, I was amazed at the stereotypes that existed within P&G itself among our different European nationalities. We had a retreat, the purpose of which was to express openly how we felt about one another—Italians, French, Germans—and I was blown away by the stereotypical negative views people had of one another. How little we understood one another. We knew that couldn't stand. We knew we had to work across countries to take advantage of our best advertising ideas and better products.

That was the beginning of my journey to see the importance of people knowing each other as individual people. Lots of learning followed. For example, several African Americans told me candidly they felt there were having to use too much energy in fitting in. A diversity training session called for me to play the role of a black female worker who was supervised by a white male with two negative biases against people who worked for him: women and African Americans. During that 30-minute role play, I almost reached the point of acting out my frustrations against the woman who played the male supervisor, even though she was someone I knew and admired well!

By the time I was appointed CEO in 1995, the importance of the company's diversity was clear and measurable—something I knew we had to prioritize. The CEOs who preceded me, John Smale and Ed Artzt, had done just that. I and CEOs who have succeeded me continued that emphasis as a vital priority for the future of the business.

The experiences continued. I was seeing in one context after another the benefit of diversity, equity, and inclusion, and also how intentional we needed to be to overcome stereotypes—what we're now calling implicit (unconscious) biases—that can lead us to fail to see people as individuals rather than some class on which we have pinned a label. Despite some progress, we still remain a long way from being where we should be in taking advantage of diversity and inclusion, particularly in the development and advancement of under-represented populations.

The question now isn't whether diversity, equity, and inclusion are strategic imperatives; they are. The question is how we more consistently make good on delivering them. With this book, I believe Janet and Vincent have defined a whole new pathway to achieving the diversity, equity, and inclusion we seek. They have taken their search to break down the barriers to diversity, equity, and inclusion into a vital new territory—the human brain. They have learned that as human beings, we all have what we call implicit (unconscious) biases. They've explored key factors influencing how people behave—the impact of nature, nurture, and biology—and the mindsets that can lead to biased behavior. Most importantly, Janet and Vincent have discovered that invoking the "power of the pause" before we act instinctively can result in intrinsically inclusive behavior when we recognize—and own—our implicit, unconscious biases. We've long realized that diversity, equity, and inclusion will not progress on automatic pilot. There are too many other competing demands. Diversity, equity, and inclusion require continued and vigorous leadership from top management and studious application of learning to do better. This book is a rich source of such learning. That's why I recommend you read it.

PROLOGUE

Former Global Chief Diversity and Inclusion Officer,
Procter & Gamble, and President, End-to-End Packaging
and Transformation

As global chief diversity and inclusion officer at Procter & Gamble, I have experienced for myself the power of diversity, equity, and inclusion (DEI) to efficiently and successfully open and expand markets, and grow our business in the United States and around the world.

I have also come to understand that while we can impose diversity—equity and inclusion must be cultivated. Neither is a natural "go-to" state for the human brain. That's not how most of us are wired. Our brains have evolved to keep us safe. That means being suspicious of people who seem different. Thus, our instinct is to avoid the "other," and move toward people who look like, act like, and overall seem more like us. And the higher the stakes in the relationship, the more the brain steers us toward those it thinks are most safe, most comfortable—i.e., most like us. So, it only makes sense that the further up the corporate ladder you go, the harder DEI becomes to achieve.

Which is why despite all our DEI gains in the last several decades, we—as a global marketplace—have barely put a dent in diversity in leadership. In fact, recently in some industries, the homogeneity has gotten worse. And we in the DEI profession have been at a loss as to how to change that.

Until now.

What Janet Reid and Vincent Brown have put forth in *Intrinsic Inclusion: Rebooting the Biased Brain* is nothing short of revolutionary. By looking at DEI through the lens of neuroscience and social psychology, they ask questions about how we can break out of old biases—even those we are unaware of—and begin to develop brains that lean more toward inclusiveness, brains that are more intrinsically inclusive.

The information in this book creates a new set point for dialogue among DEI professionals—one that places the focus on the individual. I invite those who are CDIOs, CEOs, COOs, and all C-suite individuals—as well as anyone else interested in opening their own mind—to first read this work and then get involved in this effort to move both the science and the outcomes for DEI forward.

INTRODUCTION

One Simple Question

by JANET B. REID, Ph.D.
and VINCENT R. BROWN

" Is there a way to reboot our brains so we're naturally motivated to move toward those who aren't like us, instead of away from them?"

That question, seemingly impromptu when first posed in the fall of 2015, had grown out of years of frustration. Today, as polarization within our society only continues to swell, answering it becomes even more urgent.

For thirty years, we assisted corporations across the globe in implementing strong diversity, equity, and inclusion (DEI) programs. As business partners along with three others, we'd taken our firm, Global Novations (formerly Global Lead Management Consulting), from an idea over coffee to the largest DEI consultancy in the world. Always at the cutting edge of strategic thinking, our services and learning programs were in high demand when we sold the firm to one of world's largest executive search and leadership development companies in 2012.

By most conventional measures, we'd been successful.

But after the sale, we used our two-year non-compete period to take stock. Had we made the difference we'd wanted to? Was DEI where we thought it would be thirty years on?

Honestly, our answer was "No."

While our firm—and the DEI profession as a whole—had made impressive and measurable contributions to workplace diversity, in reality, the most meaningful strides remained limited to entry-level and middle management. One common (but not the only) measure of progress is to note the status of the racial/ethnic minority and female populations within organizations. Both populations were—and still are—barely represented in the executive ranks and hard to find in the boardroom.

When it comes to the C-suite, DEI hit a wall decades ago. And though we and many others who work in corporations had put years of effort into scaling that wall, we were barely off the ground. Many of the strategies we'd devised were working and necessary and needed to remain in place for continued progress, but they weren't sufficient. Something more was needed.

But what? What were we missing here?

That question ate at us, finding its way into every discussion we had. As soon as the non-compete ended, we both went back into DEI full tilt—each opening our own boutique consulting firms and joining with others to form a consortium of seasoned senior diversity, equity, and inclusion consultants.

INTRINSIC INSPIRATION

By early 2015, Vincent found himself fielding more and more requests to help high-performing teams fully leverage their diversity. Around the same time, new findings in cultural competencies, biases, trust building, emotional intelligence, and other psychosocial phenomena were coming across his desk. He incorporated some of the more relevant information into his programs.

Right from the start, the results were encouraging. By simply bringing awareness to the science behind deep-seated motivations and beliefs, people were better able to lift their once-limiting thought patterns, or at the very least to see them in a new light.

These first little successes made both of us even more curious about what brain science might hold for diversity, equity, and inclusion—especially when it came to the executive level. So, we decided to put our heads together once again and find out more.

At the start of this new commitment, Janet came across an article on motivation that referred to self-determination theory and the notion of intrinsic motivation—doing something because you want to, not for reward or to avoid punishment. It made her think about people she and Vincent had worked with in corporations over the years who didn't need a reason to be inclusive. They naturally filled their lives and workspaces with all types of people and ideas. It was just the way they were. But what made them that way? Why are some people able to work with others different from themselves with ease? And was it possible to learn to be intrinsically motivated toward inclusion?

HALLS OF WONDER

That fall, Janet was touring the Neurological Institute at the Wexner Medical Center at The Ohio State University (OSU), where she was a former university trustee. Inside the institute's labs, researchers were working on what would strike most of us as the stuff of science fiction: trans-cranial magnets to treat mood disorders, analyzing brain patterns to allow people with epilepsy to predict seizures, a wearable diagnostic device that could pinpoint the cause of back pain.

Her guide through these halls of wonder was no less than renowned neurosurgeon and director of the institute at that time, Dr. Ali Rezai. Today, Dr. Rezai heads the Rockefeller Neuroscience Institute at West Virginia University. If his name sounds familiar, it might be because in the spring of 2016 it appeared in about every major media outlet, including on the front page of *The New York Times*. Dr. Rezai is part of the team that made it possible for a patient with quadriplegia to move his hand and fingers with his thoughts. (It's okay to take a moment and read that sentence again.)

Dr. Rezai had implanted in the patient's brain a neuroprosthetic device, developed by the team, that allowed the man's thoughts to bypass his severed nerves and reopen communication between his brain and his body. It was unprecedented.

Even before that game-changing accomplishment, Dr. Rezai was well known for his pioneering work with neuromodulation and the brain pacemaker. His research in this area has resulted in successful treatments for Parkinson's disease, depression, obsessive-compulsive disorder, and traumatic brain injury. Currently, he and his team are testing neuromodulation in the treatment of migraine headaches, addiction, Alzheimer's disease, obesity, post-traumatic stress disorder, and autism, among other conditions.

That afternoon, as Janet witnessed one marvel after the next, she couldn't help thinking of the current state of DEI. When we started our firm in the 1990s, the conventional wisdom said that all businesses needed in order to achieve diversity was to bring in a diverse population of workers and train them, and eventually the cream would rise to the top. Well, it took much more than hiring a diverse population, and we are proud of what our firm accomplished; but frankly, we thought we'd be further along by now.

Reasons, theories, and contributing factors as to why corporations cannot or do not diversify at the executive level abound. In truth, it's complicated. But as Janet walked along with Dr. Rezai that day, she started to think it cannot be more complicated than predicting an epileptic seizure, or designing a pacemaker for the brain, or getting a thought to bypass a severed nerve and make a once-paralyzed limb move. And she thought about self-determination theory and intrinsic motivation.

So, she turned to Dr. Rezai and asked: "Is there a way to reboot our brains so we're naturally motivated to move toward those who aren't like us, instead of away from them?"

He thought for a moment. And he said, "I don't know, but let's explore it."

We took Dr. Rezai up on his offer.

MERGING FIELDS

Dr. Rezai recruited some of the finest minds in the fields of social neuroscience and its sister science, social psychology. We gathered corporate colleagues currently working in DEI, and we all came together for the first-ever Neuroscience of Diversity and Inclusion Workshop on the OSU campus in the spring of 2016. The meeting's goal was to begin a conversation on how neuroscience might move DEI forward faster.

The workshop started with researchers sharing their findings—some yet to be published—on pertinent areas such as implicit bias, various aspects of stereotyping, types of empathy, how our brains form impressions, and how syncing our physical bodies (e.g., marching in time) can generate empathy. All of which we'll take a close look at in the coming chapters.

Researchers then joined the corporate executives at small tables for discussion. Immediately, questions flew, thoughts were exchanged, concepts formed. Executives gained insights into the hard-wired, psychological, and biological challenges of achieving diversity, equity, and inclusion. Scientists delighted in considering their research in terms of real-life problems. The energy was palpable.

We both knew right there that DEI was entering a new phase.

In its first phase, back in the early 1990s, diversity was seen as a legal and compliance issue for the most part, and that was it. If we had twenty-five people in a learning program, maybe five even knew what diversity was. Over the decades, as workplaces diversified, we and others helped clients realize that diversity improved their company's performance in quantifiable ways, and DEI left the compliance arena and became part of a prudent business strategy.

Thus, our firm and its consulting services grew in demand. We advised organizations both large and small, including most Fortune 100 and 500 companies. More notably, we helped develop diversity, equity, and inclusion strategies that had measures and accountabilities and that linked to the overall corporate strategy. As part of those strategies, we facilitated and presented DEI seminars and classes for thousands of people. Corporate diversity councils sought our guidance. We also co-authored two books, *Diversity Councils That Work* and *The Phoenix Principles: Leveraging Inclusion to Transform Your Company*, which took readers step-by-step through proven DEI practices.

Obviously, we no longer had to convince anyone of DEI's value. Everyone clearly understood that diversity made sense on multiple levels. And corporate leaders were sincere in their desire to achieve diversity, equity, and inclusion for their organizations. Yet, despite the awareness, the desire, all the effort, and the increased diversity in lower and middle management, diversity among corporate senior ranks remained elusive.

That is, until the OSU workshop made our next steps clear.

We realized we had spent our careers working with the software or nurture side of DEI—developing systems and facilitating learning. Now neuroscience was handing us the means to look at the hardware or the nature side—brain functioning—and integrate that into what we do. Though our knowledge of neuroscience was rudimentary in that moment (to say the least), we could see that within that science was the understanding that we needed to take DEI to the next level, to reboot the biased brain.

SCIENCE-INSPIRED SOLUTIONS

Motivated by all we had learned, we formally began our own research into what neuroscience had to reveal about the promise of DEI and our challenges as human beings in achieving it. We returned to the fields of social neuroscience and social psychology. We explored the various facets of the human brain along with the experts and learned how these facets work together to tell us whom we like, whom we trust, whom we choose, and why. We worked on the issue of intrinsic motivation, asking experts all along the way whether neural pathways could be changed so people would be more likely to embrace "the other" and value differences.

Some of what we found affirmed things we previously felt to be true and revealed why many of our current DEI learning programs and practices do work.

The biggest hurdles we found were that so many of our brain processes occur at an unconscious level, and that, as human beings, we are wired to select for our in-group. The good news is there are things we as individuals can do not only to override that wiring, but also to possibly change it to better serve us, and thus align our decisions with our diversity, equity, and inclusion goals.

Based on the knowledge we gathered, we have developed and introduced new DEI learning programs, strategies, and systems more in tune with our natural brain processes— working with them, not against them.

A Book of Questions More Than Answers

We also decided to write this book to share what we have learned so far, as well as invite more voices and experiences (i.e., your voice and experiences) into the conversation.

Obviously, understanding how we think, why we think, and what we think can prove useful in every area of our lives. However, to best discuss and illustrate the information we've collected, we chose to frame it in the arena where we've had the most experience with it: business. But to be clear, these insights have had a profound impact on our day-to-day lives, and we encourage you to apply whatever you discover here in any area of your own life where you think it can be an enhancement.

The book begins with exploring the state of DEI in the business world today and what we stand to lose by not finding a way to break through our very natural resistance to "the other." We present the ideal DEI state—the one every business puts in its DEI mission statement but rarely attains—and show how and why if it were realized it would take corporations to new heights of innovation and profitability.

We then look into the science that explains why our brains and our biology reject this ideal state, even when we consciously say we want it and invest great effort trying to achieve it in our workplaces. With our biology and brain functioning in mind, we lay out what businesses can do to encourage an ideal DEI environment through encouraging intrinsic motivation. We wed those aims to new tactics and learning programs we're currently using in the field and introduce some strategies we've learned about but have yet to try.

Our book *The Phoenix Principles: Leveraging Inclusion to Transform Your Company* was born out of our own field experiences. This book takes that foundational knowledge and joins it with cognitive research to produce new findings and new directions for DEI. These are early days in our journey to discovering how neuroscience can inform and support DEI efforts.

As you'll soon find, this is a book of questions more than answers, and we invite you, the reader, to join the conversation. In the last chapter, you'll find a host of ways to be part of what we hope will become a learning community.

Enjoy the book. We look forward to exchanging thoughts, ideas, experiences, and questions with you soon.

1

THE STAKES

I think that if we understood our cognitive limitations in the same way that we understand our physical limitations, even though they don't stare us in the face in the same way, we could design a better world.

—DAN ARIELY[1]

What if something as small as a grain of rice could be put near the spine to prevent post-surgery pain, eliminating the need for opioids? What if a microchip implanted in the mouth could end migraine headaches? What if virtual reality could alleviate post-traumatic stress disorder, ease the phantom pain of a missing limb, or allow someone to experience being a different race or gender?

These aren't "someday" miracles; they are possibilities being tested in labs right now.

In the last two decades, the fields of neuroscience and social psychology have exploded with insight and innovation. Huge advances in neuroimaging have allowed scientists to watch the brain function in real time—to see thoughts form, emotions happen, and impressions take shape in amazing detail. Aided by these once-unimaginable images, technologies, and procedures are being explored to interrupt, redirect, or change some of the well-worn, evolution-based brain patterns that no longer serve us well as human beings in a modern society.

In those same decades, diversity, equity, and inclusion (DEI)—our field of expertise—has had some trouble finding results at the executive level. While the workforce in general has achieved and benefited greatly from growing diversity, upper leadership in the vast majority of organizations remains stubbornly homogenous. Despite the DEI profession's best efforts, approximately 94 percent of Fortune 500 CEOs are white men—and that percentage has remained pretty steady for years. That's not healthy for business. And it's not healthy for society.

But what if we were to apply neuroscience and neuroimaging to DEI? What if we could peek inside our heads and see what goes on when we meet, interview, or are interviewed by someone who is very different from us? What if we could see which brain synapses fire when we are asked to collaborate with, mentor, be led by, or hire that person? And what if we then could change our own reaction to achieve the response we desire? What if we could create new neural pathways and reboot our brains for inclusiveness? What if we could encourage the changes in our body chemistry that help to establish trust and create respectful empathy, leading to more real human connections and inclusive behaviors?

These are not "someday" questions either. These are questions we asked of, and are continuing to pose to, leading researchers in both social neuroscience and social psychology. And though science has just begun to share its promise in this area, the answers we've already found have brought great light to the reasons behind DEI's successes and our current challenges, giving us a host of new ideas and providing science-inspired directions for building on the progress we've made.

WHAT IS DEI?

When we talk of diversity, the two categories that typically come to mind are race and gender. But optimal workplace diversity embraces a full range of similarities and differences, such as age, educational background, physical capabilities, family and cultural derivation, sexual orientation, gender identity, recreational preference, and socioeconomic status, to name a few. The best teams also work toward diversity in cognitive preferences—how we like to receive and give information, problem-solve, communicate, and engage with others. Basically, any feature that broadens the experience and perspective of a group should be sought after. Part of recognizing diversity is also recognizing the underlying similarities among all people on which we can begin to build meaningful relationships.

While essential, achieving diversity itself is not enough. Equity is the process of providing everyone, in a fair manner, what is needed to be successful and then consistently rewarding that success. Diversity is the prerequisite to inclusion, which is where the true riches are. Inclusion is leveraging the power of a group's diversity to attain a common goal or objective. It is not about people blending in—corporate "fit" and assimilation are yesterday's thinking. It's appreciating differences and similarities and creating an environment that encourages people to bring their unique capabilities to the table for the organization's benefit.

DEI Is Non-negotiable

Despite its challenges, DEI only continues to grow in its importance to an organization's successful strategy:

Josh Bersin, principal and founder of Bersin by Deloitte, named DEI a top priority for 2016 in *Forbes*.[2]

DEI was named one of the top strategic issues for institutional governing boards in 2016 and 2017 by the Association of Governing Boards of Universities and Colleges.[3]

Eighty technology companies and counting have signed a White House pledge created under the Obama administration to diversify their workforces.[4]

Even former CIA Director Michael Hayden is quoted in an intra-agency study on diversity in leadership as saying, "That diversity is mission critical is no longer a debatable proposition—if it ever was."[5]

None of this is surprising. The economy in which we work and live is global. And as technology and communications continue to advance, our world only gets smaller. Sameness is by definition limiting: one gender, one race, one culture, one perspective. It's not exactly conducive to solving multifaceted problems and creating competitive strategies in a global marketplace. If businesses want to remain relevant, let alone competitive, they need a workforce—including their leadership—that reflects the world they serve.

They know it. We all know it.

So, businesses and organizations rightly have invested billions of dollars and significant employee time to create diversity and promote equity and inclusion. DEI is now standard in most corporate mission and values statements. There are DEI strategic plans complete with accountability measures. Serious recruitment, retention, and advancement programming for minority populations are common, along with mentoring and sponsoring initiatives. Most companies offer broad-scale DEI learning experiences. And employees are intentionally made aware of the business, customer, shareholder, moral, and other practical rationales for DEI.

These efforts have made a difference and helped organizations prosper. Yet, despite all this, full integration of DEI into the most senior leadership ranks remains an issue.

NEUROSCIENCE: THE GAME CHANGER

But neuroscience and neuroimaging have now given us an inside track. They have allowed us into the brain, so we can see its natural, often unconscious responses when confronted with diversity or asked to be inclusive. We can now consider bias and stereotyping, as well as people's need to belong, from the brain's perspective.

We can also consider that we change each other's biology when we interact. If our brains judge the person we're talking with to be a friend or an in-group member, we now know that they signal the release of serotonin, causing our bodies to relax and produce a sense of well-being. That chemical helps us to feel an automatic empathy toward the other person and to give them the benefit of the doubt. But when our brains judge the person as an out-group member or potential foe, adrenaline is released along with corresponding fight, flight, or freeze reactions. We become hyperalert; our heart rate, blood pressure, and breathing increase; our eyes narrow; and our hearing becomes more sensitive. We become driven by emotion rather than reason. Of course, the level of these reactions is in proportion to the level of comfort or threat our brains sense. But amazingly, all of this often happens within seconds and without us being consciously aware of it. Understanding this physiological reality alone, of course, changes the way we think about strategies for bringing diverse populations together.

This more complete, behind-the-scenes picture of human interaction is helping us develop new, even more effective DEI strategies that use and, when possible, take advantage of our natural thought processes and our brain and body functions. Most importantly, the science has shown us how best to help people understand, check, and then manage their behaviors toward "the other" from the inside out. Empowered with that intrinsic motivation, they can more easily realize and benefit from diversity, equity, and inclusion in their organizations and their lives.

As it has done for so many fields in recent years, neuroscience has breathed new life into our DEI efforts and put us at the vanguard of a new path forward. One with the opportunity to finally break through those stubborn barriers—the ones in our own heads—that have kept us from the fully diverse, equitable, and inclusive environment we not only want but also need to progress in our businesses and as a society.

2

WE ARE ALL BIASED...
YET WIRED TO CONNECT

We have met the enemy and he is us.

—POGO THE POSSUM
(Walt Kelly, cartoonist)[6]

Human beings are social animals. We are driven to connect with others; in fact, our very survival depends on our ability to form relationships. But to be human is also to be biased and tribal—to prefer those we perceive as like us and to be wary of those we view as different. That's not a judgment on humankind. It's a fact. And one that both social psychology (the study of our behavior and thought processes as we relate, think about relating, or imagine relating to other people) and social neuroscience (which looks at our physiological responses to social interactions) attempt to explain.

Before we began researching this book, honestly, we didn't fully comprehend how organic bias is to the human condition and how essential it is to our navigating our everyday world. That said, if we are to move diversity, equity, and inclusion forward, we must not only accept that we all bring bias to many of the decisions we make, but also understand our biases and how they work so we can begin to manage them, instead of being managed by them.

WE ARE ALL BIASED

Dr. Russell Fazio, professor of social psychology at The Ohio State University and a trailblazer in the field of attitudes and social cognition, explains bias simply and non-judgmentally as "a preference for or against something, someone, or some perspective."[7] Biases develop from our culture, socialization, and life experiences. For instance, if your mother made a great meatloaf, and you enjoyed eating it, you probably have a positive bias toward meatloaf in general. If she made horrible meatloaf, and you were forced to finish every bite, you probably have a negative bias against it. If your siblings hated it, too, they culturally reinforced your negative bias.

It's both that simple and that much a part of us.

Biases develop over time and strengthen through repetition. Whenever your mother served meatloaf, your neurons—nerve cells that transmit information—traveled a pathway in your brain from stimuli (the meatloaf) to your response ("Yum" or "Yuck"). The more times your neurons made that trip, the more established that neural pathway and your bias became. For example, if you had meatloaf every Sunday, you are more likely to have a stronger bias, whether positive or negative, than someone who encountered the dish less often.

Over the course of our lives, our brains have paved such neural pathways for almost everything we regularly encounter. Needless to say, we are more likely to have a positive bias toward people and things we know well, feel part of, and are comfortable with, such as our family, our nationality, our race, our generation, our religion, or our politics. We tend to be negatively biased against—i.e., dislike or be suspicious of—people and things we are unfamiliar with, have had bad experiences with, or are told not to like by those we trust, such as different cultural traditions, people of different races, rival teams, opposing politics, and many other descriptions.

And that is true for every one of us. Bias is not biased.

WE ALL CAN STEREOTYPE

While bias speaks to a personal preference, a stereotype is more a preconceived notion. The *Dictionary of Psychology* defines a stereotype as "a fixed, over-generalized belief about a particular group or class of people."[8] Stereotypes can be positive or negative and include any number of characteristics, such as: New Yorkers talk fast, Southerners are polite, men like sports, women like fashion, and people who wear glasses are smart and like to read.

Like biases, stereotypes can develop from personal experience, but most are cultural, passed to us almost by osmosis through our families, our religion, and our communities. Sometimes our media reinforce them. For instance, mothers on most sitcoms today are portrayed as working outside the home—something that wasn't true of sitcom moms a generation ago—but they still are likely to be the family member shown doing housework and cooking dinner, while fathers grill, take care of the cars, and forget their anniversaries, all reflecting modern societal stereotypes.

Our brains use stereotypes to classify people quickly. All we need to know or assume is one thing about a person—skin color, age, gender, clothes, accent, street address, religious affiliation—and our brains automatically place them in a group and bestow our version of that group's characteristics on them until proven otherwise.

The famous study "Are Emily and Greg More Employable than Lakisha and Jamal?" demonstrates this human proclivity. Five thousand resumes were sent out in response to 1,300 want ads. The resumes were identical except for the applicants' names; some of the applicants had typical Euro-American names, and some had names more commonly associated with African Americans. At the study's conclusion, the resumes with Euro-American sounding names received 50 percent more interview requests.[9] Based solely on a name, resume readers assigned racial stereotypes to the applicants and then factored those traits into their decision on whom to interview.

We'd like to point out here that simply producing a diverse slate of candidates alone is not enough to advance, let alone reap the rewards of diversity, equity, and inclusion. Even the most diverse candidate pool doesn't guarantee that a non-majority member candidate will be judged by whomever is doing the hiring as the best person for the job. No slate can stop bias or an inclination to stereotype and our natural preference for those who are more like us. It's how our brains have evolved to work. Even if a non-majority candidate were hired from that diverse slate, bias and an inclination to stereotype can still limit our ability to be inclusive, undermining performance all around.

A diverse slate is not the objective. A diverse workforce in an inclusive environment is. And to get there, you have to actually hire different types of people and have an organizational atmosphere they feel part of, so they stay and contribute.

IMPLICIT BIAS

The well-worn neural pathways that form our biases and stereotypes eventually create regular patterns and schemas in our thought processes. Feelings and emotions attach to these patterns. When our brains associate a person with a preconceived attitude (bias), our emotions whisk our neurons to the predetermined judgment, often before we're aware it has happened. Dr. Fazio labels this everyday phenomenon—and it is an everyday phenomenon—an "automatically activated attitude."[10] It is often referred to as implicit bias.

For instance, let's say your father went to the Pennsylvania State University and always talked about how great the school was. Growing up, you loved hearing his college stories. You also love your father. In your mind, he was a successful, smart guy.

At work, you find yourself interviewing a job candidate who graduated from Penn State. Simple exposure to your bias's stimuli or the mere hint of it (the mention of the school) triggers your deep bias's pattern or schema ("My dad went there; that's a great school; I love my dad; he's a smart guy."), and that sends your neurons on their emotionally charged, predetermined path toward judgment and a decision. ("This candidate is a smart guy; I like him; I'd like to hire him.") Only then does your brain go searching for some convincing facts to support your judgment (great resume, good experience). And while in the end you believe your decision to hire the Penn State grad isn't based on his alma mater alone, the fact remains that you were influenced in a positive direction toward him in ways you were not aware of and thus did not account for in your deliberations or your consideration of other candidates.

There are a few schools of thought around such unacknowledged bias. Dr. Fazio uses the term "implicit" because he believes we know how we feel about something, though we are not always fully conscious that we are using that attitude as a factor in our decisions.[11] Other researchers use the term "unconscious bias," believing we are completely unaware that our preference for or against something even exists. Regardless of our level of consciousness around our biases or the term we use, the effect and impact are the same. We make decisions without full awareness of our underlying attitude's influence on those decisions. And that is a problem. It is also something that researchers believe we can work on and change. We can take back control of our thought processes, but we have to make an effort to do so. (More on that later in the book.)

Clearly, permitting implicit bias to determine our judgment or behaviors as we relate to other people can have very serious implications for our lives and our businesses. Besides preventing us from seeing the objective facts of a situation and the actual skills and talents—or lack thereof—of the person in front of us, it can undermine our goals and desires.

After all, for decades companies have touted their commitment to diversifying their workforce, including leadership. Strategies and policies to realize that commitment are designed. Education is procured. Human resources departments recruit diverse candidate pools. But when it comes down to the selection of executives and higher, the decision makers consistently choose others like themselves, going against their own directive.

If asked why, they won't say it's because they prefer people like themselves. They don't even consciously think that. What the leadership might say is that they reviewed the facts, and in the end they chose the best person for the job, regardless of gender or race. "Sally was very competitive, but in the end, Jim's experience at XYZ made him the better candidate." And they believe it.

WE ALL PREFER OUR IN-GROUP

By the way, we all prefer people like ourselves. In our experience, companies with African American CEOs tend to have more African Americans in leadership roles. Companies with Caucasian CEOs tend to have more Caucasians in leadership roles. And the same often goes for gender, religion, or any other category a CEO identifies himself or herself by. Left to their own thought processes, most people are going to hire and promote in their own image.

And when that very human tendency isn't acknowledged and managed, businesses lose out, because the person selected isn't likely to support the goals of, or move the company forward in, its DEI mission. Again, this is not a judgment;

it is how our brains and implicit bias work when unrealized and unchallenged.

Scientists theorize that our inclination toward stereotyping and bias is part of our innate drive to sort people into "in-groups," those we feel a kinship to, and "out-groups," those we think of as the "other" and therefore dislike or fear. In-group determination can be and, at first, often is based on self-defining traits—family, race, nationality, religion, political belief, socioeconomic status. But that determination is surprisingly fluid.

While you'd think we'd carefully deliberate and base in reason those we accept into our in-group and those we place in our out-group, you'd be wrong. A wide variety of experiments show that we make these decisions quickly and base them on anything and everything, and that they are malleable—meaning we change in-group/out-group status as circumstances change. In fact, in an aside during an interview, Dr. Baldwin Way, assistant professor of psychology at The Ohio State University, whose work focuses on social neurochemistry (how psychological factors affect the immune systems and vice versa), told us about dividing volunteers into two groups for one of his projects that had nothing to do with the in-group/out-group phenomenon. He lined them up, had them count off from one to twenty, and asked them to split into odds and evens. Within five minutes, he noted, his volunteers were already displaying in-group/out-group behaviors and making a competition out of the experiment.[12] Remember, the group members' only commonality stemmed from their placement in line—odd or even.

Even when so shallowly rooted, the in-group/out-group status we assign is meaningful because it has significant implications for how we think about and regard other people.

Different parts of our brains become activated, depending on that assignment.[13] Our brains actually give positive traits to in-group members and negative traits to those whom are placed in the out-group.[14] As the chart below shows, in-group members are assigned both high trust and competence, and thus are highly valued with no basis in evidence. And while an out-group member may sometimes be either trustworthy or competent, they are never regarded as both, though they can be—and often are—considered both incompetent and untrustworthy.[15]

THE MIND CATEGORIZES IN- AND OUT-GROUPS

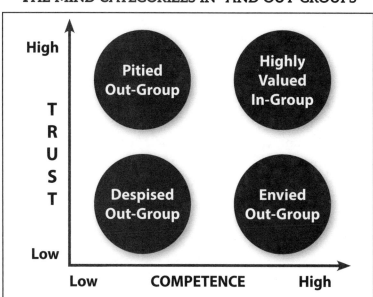

Adapted From: Douglas S. Massey, *Categorically Unequal: The American Stratification System*, New York: Russell Sage Foundation, 2007.

As an added bonus for in-group members, when a brain registers trust, it releases oxytocin—often described as the social-bonding hormone. It's the same hormone that mothers produce as they nurse their babies, providing a calm, connected feeling—which, of course, enables inclusive behaviors. Distrust, on the other hand, produces "fight-or-flight" chemicals, causing stress and high alert in the body.

One of the more famous examples of in-group/out-group manipulation occurred in 1968, two days after the assassination of Dr. Martin Luther King Jr. In response to a student's question about prejudice, third grade teacher Jane Elliott divided her class into those with blue eyes and those with brown or green eyes.

On the first day of the experiment, she placed paper armbands on the blue-eyed children. She told the children that brown eyes indicate intellectual superiority. And she even gave them a bogus scientific reason why: she said brown-eyed people have more melanin, and that makes them smarter.

Almost immediately, the brown-eyed children acted superior. Even brown-eyed students who had previously been shy or slower acted bolder and were more outspoken, Stephen Bloom reported in his article "Lessons of a Lifetime" for *Smithsonian* in 2005. They ridiculed their blue-eyed classmates and assigned negative traits to them—saying they were lazy and dirty, and spread disease—all classic accusations from in-group members to their out-group counterparts. Also worth noting is that once-confident blue-eyed children began struggling with academic tasks in which they'd previously shown proficiency.

The next school day, Elliott switched the group's status— the blue-eyed children were now superior. Without hesitation, they took on heightened-rank behaviors, though reportedly they were a little kinder to their brown-eyed less-thans, having recently experienced oppression themselves. Still, these children quickly identified with their in-group, assigning their group's supposed qualities to themselves, whether deserved or not, and felt disdain for out-group members who just a few days earlier had been their friends.

When the experiment was over, so was the divide. The children dropped the blue-eyed/brown-eyed designations, thus demonstrating how alterable in-group/out-group identifications can be.[16]

The in-group/out-group dynamic exemplifies the many calculations going on in our brains at lightning speed at the moment we encounter, interact with, or think about someone. It also demonstrates that our judgment of another is not necessarily fixed, as our initial bias and stereotyping might lead us to believe. With a passing suggestion or a change of a team jersey, our minds make judgments about others, without awareness or consideration, drawing consequential conclusions—both positive and negative. Realizing this can be game-changing when it comes to diversity, equity, and inclusion.

Obviously, our allegiance to in-group members—such as family, longtime friends, or a cultural group we strongly identify with—is not so easily manipulated. But for less intense relationships, such as work relationships, bias can be and is overridden by creating the smallest sense of belonging (odds/evens; blue eyes/brown eyes) even if only for a moment in a certain circumstance. Once we understand this, we can use it to DEI's advantage.

WE ARE ALSO WIRED TO CONNECT

Our drive to connect and belong is just as strong, if not stronger in some ways, as our drive to judge and shun. This shouldn't be surprising. Our ability to cooperate is often credited for our species' success. And cooperation demands connection.

Think about the first thing you do when you meet someone. Chances are you ask your new acquaintance questions about themselves: "What do you do? Where did you grow up? Read any good books lately?" Instinctively, you are searching for something about them you can relate to, so you can begin to build a relationship, move that person to your in-group, and hopefully belong to their in-group as well.

Social psychology calls this kernel of social connection "mere belonging." Steven Spencer, professor of social psychology at The Ohio State University, whose studies focus on motivation and the self, explained it to us as a "yoked condition"—a subject, interest, or experience that ties one person to another. Or he suggests thinking about it as a Venn diagram. We instinctively work to get the other person's circle to overlap ours.[17]

The more dissimilar the person seems from us, obviously, the harder our brains must work to find the traits that make those circles overlap. And frankly, our brains don't like hard work or busy multitasking. Unless otherwise instructed or rebooted, they take the path of least resistance to preserve energy. So, if there's a choice, your brain is going to point you toward the person in the room who is most like you to get your connection fix. That is why at networking events, people tend to hang out with people from their own company or people they already know, though the whole point of the gathering is to expand their network.

BIAS ISN'T BAD

As averse as we like to think we are to bias, we wouldn't make it through the day without it. Bias, stereotyping, and in-group/out-group status all evolved over human history to help us function in the world.

Scientists believe in-group/out-group bias developed as a survival instinct. Since humans began roaming the Earth, those outside their tribe or group posed the threat of war or disease. Their lives depended on their ability to quickly determine whether someone was a danger. Thus, suspicion of the foreigner—meaning anyone who does not look like, act like, or hold the same values as the tribe—became a regular thought pattern and eventually an automatically activated attitude.

These ancient "out-group" triggers are still active in our brains today. Upon first sight, before a person even speaks, we size them up and make judgments. In a virtual reality experiment where subjects saw either an angry-looking or a smiling man walking toward them, researchers found that the subjects' brains instinctively read, assessed, and reacted to the man. Different parts of the brain were activated, depending on whether the subject detected dominance or affiliation.[18]

While we might not face a constant threat of war or disease from foreign marauders these days, our innate ability to determine a threat in an instant still protects us. When the hair on the back of our neck stands up, when something just feels off about a person or a situation, or when we turn our face away when someone sneezes, that's our brain recognizing threat and setting off our body's warning systems before we even register what's happening. Sometimes this Spidey sense is uncannily accurate. But it can also be set off by unfounded bias toward, and stereotyping of, an out-group member.

RELIEVING THE TENSION

As for bias and stereotyping, our brains process millions of pieces of information per second. Yet, it's believed we are only conscious of several dozen pieces at a time at best. Bias and stereotyping organize this information and make decisions for us based on patterns we've established over a lifetime. If we were to consider every piece of stimuli that comes at us in a day and make a conscious decision, we'd be paralyzed. Bias and stereotyping make our lives efficient and manageable.

For millennia, this tension between inclusion and exclusion within us broke toward negative bias and stereotyping for our safety and survival. But as we have moved from a tribal to a global existence, our bias toward exclusion limits us and might even endanger us. It definitely endangers our businesses.

When asked by famed journalist Edward R. Murrow what the most detestable word in the English language was, poet and writer Carl Sandburg replied, "Exclusive." He explained, "When you're exclusive, you shut out a more or less large range of humanity from your mind and heart, from your understanding of them."[19]

Exclusion doesn't serve us in the twenty-first century. We consciously know this. There isn't a CEO in the world today who would say diversity is bad, and exclusivity is great. Yet, below that awareness, our evolution-based, emotionally driven thoughts toward "the other"—thoughts that are part of the millions of thoughts making decisions and causing our reactions without our conscious knowledge—don't care what we consciously think. They don't care what's right. They don't care about our business success. Their business is to keep us alive—and to them, that means keeping us safe from "the other."

That's the battle each of us fights in our own heads every day when it comes to DEI. No group has a monopoly on stereotypes, bias, implicit bias, or in-group/out-group preference. We are all users. We cannot turn off our bias;

it is part of us. But neuroscience now shows us that we can become more aware of it, override it when we want to, and get our brains in the right frame of mind to move our conscious agenda for diversity, equity, and inclusion forward.

3

THE IDEAL STATE OF DIVERSITY, EQUITY, AND INCLUSION

The dynamism of any diverse community depends not only on the diversity itself but on promoting a sense of belonging among those who formerly would have been considered and felt themselves outside.

—SONIA SOTOMAYOR, Associate Justice of the Supreme Court of the United States

David A. Thomas introduced the real promise of DEI to the business world in his September 2004 *Harvard Business Review* article "Diversity as Strategy." Dr. Thomas, who was a professor of organizational behavior and human resources at Harvard Business School at the time, and today president of Morehouse College, tracked, dissected, and presented lessons to be learned from IBM's pioneering, decade-spanning effort not only to diversify its ranks (executive level included), but also to use that diversity to directly inform its business strategy as the company expanded its footprint in the global marketplace.

In the article, Dr. Thomas reported that through a "significant philosophical shift—from a long tradition of minimizing differences to amplifying them," IBM was able to "seize" new opportunities. For instance, one IBM market segment—female-owned businesses worldwide—grew from $10 million in 1998 to $300 million in 2001 under this new strategy. And that was far from the only significant success.[20] Almost immediately, diversity ("inclusion," though practiced, wasn't part of the lexicon yet) started to take on new importance and urgency for organizations.

Today, most DEI mission statements carefully outline these basic objectives: 1) diversity throughout the organization, 2) a culture of inclusion to leverage that diversity, and 3) an atmosphere where people can be who they are and bring their whole selves to work every day.

WHAT THE IDEAL LOOKS LIKE

When a business meets these desired objectives—or even comes close—it gains the advantages of broad thought coupled with vigorous employee engagement. Overt bias is eliminated from the workplace. Negative stereotypes and covert biases are self-checked and self-corrected. Staff members seek relationships with colleagues, vendors, and customers who are like and unlike them, expanding both their community and opportunities. Workplace tensions and conflicts produced by fear due to differences and false judgments fall away. Minority population members of all varieties feel that they belong when using their full knowledge, experience, and talents. Pay disparities disappear, and discrimination and harassment lawsuits are no longer a worry or an expense. Most importantly, organizations are thriving and more innovative, efficient, and profitable.

Trust guarantees results—among employees, within departments, and between staff and leadership. Workers feel accepted and connected to each other and to the organization. They feel part of a team or in-group where their unique and diverse characteristics are appreciated. And that kind of belonging—along with an oxytocin boost—produces engagement.

ENGAGEMENT ON STEROIDS

Think about a time when you absolutely loved going to work. You liked your coworkers, and they liked you. There was real camaraderie.

What was the quality of your output on that job?

Take a minute, and think about it.

Now think of a time when you dreaded your job. Perhaps the work itself was okay, but the environment was lackluster. You didn't really click with your coworkers. Your boss wasn't interested in your ideas.

What was the quality of your output there?

David Hunt, a leading expert on cultural competence in healthcare and diversity-related issues in law and business, and founder of the DEI consulting firm Critical Measures, created this remarkably illustrative exercise. Not surprisingly, when we guide our workshop participants through it, the first scenario always evokes upright bodies and smiles, followed by exclamations, such as "Great," "Best work I ever did," or "Creative!" The second yields drooped shoulders, twisted faces, and quiet responses such as "Mediocre," "Awful," or "Not my best."

The power of an inclusive environment and the belonging it inspires should not be underestimated. When human beings feel part of something, they give themselves to it. And when they are accepted as their authentic selves, their engagement level is on steroids. Team members feel secure, so they fearlessly add their perspective and experience, introduce ideas, try new things, and take the risk of being wrong now and then.

DIVERSITY IN SYNC

As people with diverse traits and talents work side by side in an inclusive environment, they sync up. Just like phones sync to computers—sharing information—team members share what they know, who they are, and what they value. The team's overall knowledge base, understanding, empathy, and thus processing power increase dramatically. Free-flowing interaction informs and improves every team member's output. Innovation soars. Products and services improve. Customer satisfaction grows. The organization becomes a positive, affirming place to work.

Not surprisingly, such a business attracts the best and the brightest. As inclusion continues to leverage diversity, the employees' and the company's potential expands.

FROM TRANSACTIONAL
TO TRANSFORMATIONAL

In this ideal state of diversity, equity, and inclusion, work that was once transactional becomes transformational. Team members no longer labor for a paycheck alone, doing only what's asked. Because they feel they are part of a team, they work with a desire to contribute, to positively impact the lives of their coworkers, their company, and their customers—to go beyond what's expected to what's possible.

For instance, the neuro-miracle we referenced in our introduction—the device implanted in the brain that made it possible for a paralyzed man to control his hand movements with his thoughts—came from the collaboration of multiple minds from varied disciplines: not only neurosurgeons, but also software developers, neurologists, neural engineers, electrical engineers, neuroscientists, physical therapists, and others, right down to the fortitude and capabilities of the patient himself.

Not one of them could have done it alone.

Working in tandem, each contributing their own unique experience, knowledge, and skill, the team defined the dream, created the necessary technologies, and put everything into action—working and reworking at every stage until they found success.

Interestingly enough, the project's ultimate feat— reanimating a paralyzed limb with thought via the implant—depended on the patient's brain and the computer literally syncing. According to that front-page story in the *New York Times*, at first the patient needed to see a moving avatar to prompt his neurons to send the correct message that would result in the desired movement—requiring incredible focus on his part. But as the patient and the computer continued to experiment, share information with each other, and learn the necessary brain patterns together, they found their rhythm. Eventually, the patient could achieve the movement without the avatar or as intense a focus.[21]

With awareness and purposeful concentration, our brains, too, can reboot and build up the capability to move beyond bias and be open to ideas, people, or systems that at first might feel foreign. And the rewards for such effort far outweigh the effort itself. Just look behind most modern miracles, every real push forward in an organization, and you're likely to find a team motivated to create an intrinsic sense of inclusion that allowed for the necessary transformation to occur.

DEI BECOMES THE DEFAULT

Of course, we cannot expect ourselves or our coworkers to be in the ideal DEI state every working hour of every day. As we've learned, our brains and our bodies simply don't function that way. But one very achievable and productive goal is to make diversity, equity, and inclusion our brain's default setting—defaulting toward trust versus fear, belonging instead of exclusion, engagement in place of disinterest.

What does it take to achieve this? What roadblocks do our brains need to overcome? What constitutes such an environment? What exactly does it take to keep ourselves and our coworkers moving toward that objective? What can we improve in DEI right now? And what more can we do?

4

THE CASE FOR
A NEW APPROACH

*Where Traditional DEI Approaches
Cease Working and Why*

*We thought, these injustices are so great, surely, if we just
explain them to people, they will want to fix them.*

—GLORIA STEINEM[22]

O ver the last few decades, four very rational, solid cases for cultivating DEI in the workplace arose. One: We know that DEI is smart business—and the evidence for that only multiplies over time—thus the Business Case. Two: We know that DEI is the moral (or "right") thing to do, and most people consciously want to do the right thing—thus the Right Thing to Do Case. Three: It just makes sense that having members of minority populations in leadership positions leads to more inclusive attitudes in a business's top ranks—thus the Champions to Drive Change Case. And four: Logic tells us that hiring a critical mass of a minority population translates into increased inclusion and eventually to diversity in leadership—thus the Critical Mass Case.

Using strategies based in one, two, three, or all four of these positions, DEI progressed over the decades. Until it didn't.

What we weren't so aware of—and so our current practices haven't considered—are the unforeseen forces of human psychology and even our physiology working against us, our sound arguments, and DEI itself every step of the way.

THE BUSINESS CASE FOR DEI

The Business Case for DEI has long been established. When it comes to innovation and growth, DEI is non-negotiable. Studies have identified multiple, quantifiable, and undeniable advantages to corporate diversity and inclusion, especially when present in upper management and boardrooms. Diverse and inclusive companies perform better. They are more innovative. They recognize and use special talents. They engender more employee engagement. They attract both better job candidates and better clients. And the list goes on.

But while senior executives understand all this, set strong DEI goals on paper, and certainly have the conscious intention to achieve those aims, when it comes to their leadership ranks the majority continue to promote and hire people who are like them. While this doesn't seem logical, it makes sense once you understand what's going on psychologically and neurologically.

In our brains, emotion eats reason for lunch. Emotion takes control of our thought processes, undermining our best intentions. As human beings, we can intellectually understand something, even embrace it, and then turn around and act in an opposing way. We do it every day. Knowing that half of all marriages end in divorce doesn't stop people from vowing "until death do us part"—and often more than once in a lifetime. Many people who intellectually understand that air travel is much safer than driving are still deathly afraid of flying, while they get behind the wheel without worry. And most of us are fully aware of the relationship between overeating and weight gain as we reach for that second helping.

In no-pressure, unemotional situations, we process factual information about marriage, air travel, and weight gain in our brains' frontal lobes, where reasoning and other executive-thinking tasks take place. But when we are in the midst of an emotional moment—such as anticipating the taste of more mashed potatoes—our amygdalas within our ancient brains take control, and we are driven to take the action that brings relief to our brains in the moment.

In the abstract, such as during a workshop, executives might be completely onboard with the Business Case for DEI. With space and time to work through the reasoning process, they fully comprehend that DEI makes good business sense. And when these leaders get back to their workplaces, they actually do a great job implementing DEI in departments below them. Yet, when it comes to hiring someone who will become a colleague, whom they'll have to interact with every day and whom they'll need to trust, emotion overrides reason.

A 2007 study of women in their first trimester of pregnancy—when they feel vulnerable, and their biological immune systems are on alert—found that they experience a heightened preference for their in-group.[23] New CEOs' circumstances and concerns, of course, are different from those of mothers-to-be. Yet, these leaders, too, find themselves in uncharted territory, facing new challenges, and feeling vulnerable. It's in this self-protective, emotional mental state that most select their executive team. It's no wonder they might avoid those who feel foreign and thus are drawn to and hire people who feel familiar.

The brain doesn't like risk and uncertainty, and so it will manipulate thought processes to avoid both, unless intentionally and powerfully motivated to do otherwise. While the Business Case for DEI can do a great job convincing the brain's frontal lobe that DEI is smart business, it has yet to address the formidable amygdala.

THE RIGHT THING TO DO CASE

DEI is fair and ethical. Discrimination is morally wrong.

Who could argue with that?

No one. At least not out loud in the workplace. And that's where the Right Thing to Do Case for DEI finds itself struggling against predictable brain functions. Forcing "the right thing" on people puts them on the defensive. And we all know which parts of our brain are working—and which aren't—when we feel threatened.

When a new hire is brought into an already established group, group members often experience what social psychologists call "out-group threat," meaning that just introducing someone different (out-group) into the mix challenges the in-group's status quo and thus its identity. Being big fans of the status quo, our brains find this state very uncomfortable and further intensify any biases to justify keeping that new member out. To add to the discomfort, if the established group members are aware their prejudices have surfaced, they begin to judge themselves negatively and fear the negative judgment of others. That can make it even harder for them to embrace the new hire, whom their brains blame for all this upheaval and distress.

As we've looked at, when faced with someone new, brains will try to lower any threat level by searching for commonalities on which to bond (mere belonging). But if obvious and immediate connections—such as race, age, and gender—are not present, the in-group members' brains can default to assigning out-group status to the new person, bestowing on them out-group traits—such as incompetence or untrustworthiness—further impeding the path to connection and inclusion within the work team.

In a well-known experiment, The Robbers Cave, social psychologist Muzafer Sherif demonstrated realistic conflict theory, showing that even when social commonalities are present, competition over scarce resources can produce intergroup tension. In a camp setting, over two weeks, Dr. Sherif formed two separate groups of Caucasian, Protestant, lower-middle-class, twelve-year-old boys. Once in-group bonds were established, he pitted the groups against each other in competition for prizes. The two groups—though matched in personal backgrounds—became seriously aggressive toward each other even when they weren't in formal competition.[24]

Understanding Realistic Conflict Theory, it only makes sense that the farther up the corporate ladder a person is, the higher the stakes, and thus the more intense the conflict becomes. High-level executives work in the spotlight. They are publicly judged on their work. Their jobs are valuable, few in number, harder won, often harder to replace if lost— and for most executives, their positions are integral to their identity. Their brains are always on alert for preserving their jobs, so they react strongly and negatively when anyone, especially an out-group member, is introduced into their exclusive ranks. According to Dr. Fazio, "When we view someone as a competitor, our ability to empathize with them is significantly lessened, thus reducing our ability to be inclusive."[25]

While DEI might be "the right thing to do," our brains find it stressful. Unless we deliberately intervene, our brains are not going to choose to tax themselves. So, while the Right Thing to Do Case seems obvious, when it comes to anything we perceive as scarce, being right or moral or good is not enough to overcome our brain's inclination to cling to security and fear anything or anyone it perceives as a threat.

CHAMPIONS TO DRIVE CHANGE CASE

The Champions to Drive Change Case has several members of minority populations placed in key positions throughout a company. The thinking is that through normal interaction and work activities, leadership will naturally become more inclusive, and diversity and inclusiveness will take root and grow throughout the company.

Though it makes a kind of sense on one level, our experience of it in the field has been more like this:

The CEO of a company receives a letter signed by a large group of African American leaders. They are from multiple divisions and are at different hierarchical levels, including the highest ranking African American employee in the company. The letter is well researched and contains data demonstrating a glass ceiling regarding advancement above a certain level, clear patterns of perceived bias in performance evaluations, and statistically significantly higher attrition rates versus colleagues. It also cites that no African Americans are included in corporate development or succession plans.

The CEO is alarmed and sends the letter to the Chief Diversity and Inclusion Officer (CDIO), who is African American, but not a signatory. He doesn't understand how this letter could have been written since he has been making it clear for some time that the company should increase diversity, and his efforts have been successful since there are more African Americans in key positions now than over the last five years. He tells the CDIO that she needs to "fix this problem ASAP because it has legal implications." He also tells her to bring her proposed solution to his next executive committee meeting, which includes all of his direct reports, and share how she plans to address it.

The CDIO is quite disturbed as she has consistently shared with the executive committee that inclusion—which helps to eradicate advancement barriers and unwanted attrition, among other things—does not automatically come with diversity. Inclusion requires a concerted and strategic effort. She knows that at the upcoming meeting all eyes will be on her.

She has seen the clear pattern in prior meetings with the group. When it comes to issues with African Americans, she is solely responsible for addressing them because she is African American and the CDIO. She believes this stance results from implicit bias and because senior leaders choose to abdicate their responsibility to make change. She plans to develop a comprehensive plan to mitigate all of the issues raised in the letter, but the success of the plan will depend upon the CEO and the entire senior leadership of the company taking action and being held accountable for results.

The above is a true story. And it is far from an isolated event. We've witnessed similar episodes take place in executive suites and team meeting rooms across the globe. As ridiculous and illogical as it seems, the brain registers a shared trait (e.g., race, gender, generation) between a staff member and an employee, customer, or vendor. It makes an association and concludes that the staff member is the best choice to relate to the person, no matter the issue.

Such ill-considered pairings are counterproductive, to say the least. The actual expert on the team is overlooked and discounted. All other team members abdicate their responsibility, so discussion around the topic and the ultimate solution don't benefit from diverse input. Not to mention, the champion's responsibilities double or triple, while everyone else on the team disengages. They are expected to be a spokesperson for whatever group they share a trait with. Feeling exploited and singled out, they often leave, taking the benefit of their true expertise and their unique contributions with them.

In the end, the Champions to Drive Change Case results in an exhausted "champion," disconnected leadership, and stalled DEI efforts.

THE CRITICAL MASS CASE

If businesses want diversity, they should simply hire for diversity. Set goals, meet them, and *voilà*: instant diversity. Or so the Critical Mass Case says.

But as we've learned, diversity alone is not enough. To leverage diversity's benefits, you must cultivate an environment of inclusion. Just meeting goals and throwing diverse populations together can result in fear and resentment on both sides, and eventual disengagement by those in the minority.

According to Dr. Steven Spencer, bias and stereotyping affect the thinking not only of those doing the stereotyping but also of those being stereotyped. Those being stereotyped suffer from what's known as "stereotype threat," which Dr. Spencer explains as "being both vigilant for the possibility that somebody is stereotyping you and, at the same time, not wanting to give credence to the stereotype or being stereotyped yourself."[26] He likens this state of mind to what W.E.B. Du Bois describes as "double consciousness" in his book *The Souls of Black Folk*: "This sense of always looking at one's self through the eyes of others. One ever feels his two-ness."[27]

In a series of experiments Dr. Spencer helped to conduct, one group of female subjects was told the math test they were about to take would provide evidence of gender differences, planting in their heads the cultural stereotype of women being bad at math. Another group of women took the same test but without that explanation. The women who believed the test judged their aptitude performed significantly worse than those who took the test without that inference.[28] According to Dr. Spencer, holding two opposing thoughts at once creates a challenging mental state that can result in poor performance.[29]

49

Study after study shows that the physical body revolts against stereotype threat. Blood pressure rises in the same way as when someone is aroused or anxious;[30] working memory is impaired;[31] and, of course, levels of stress-related hormones such as cortisol increase.[32]

As people go into mental battle each day with themselves, they can begin to doubt their own abilities. They may become more reactive to threat, more protective of themselves, and so less innovative and collaborative. Eventually, they often withdraw and never realize that all-important feeling of belonging or the sense of trust that comes with it.

Unfulfilled and under constant stress, many people quit their jobs. Those who don't leave are not likely to integrate well into the general population. Instead, they relieve their stress by socializing within the group they identify with, sometimes even quietly regarding all others as rivals.[33]

By not taking into account the many psychological and physiological repercussions of introducing a substantial minority population into an established majority population, the Critical Mass Case for DEI often results in alienating everyone and moving an organization further from its diversity, equity, and inclusion goals.

WORKAROUND WORKPLACE BIAS CASE

Some in DEI have concluded that all DEI efforts up until now have failed, which is not true, as the growth in diversity in the workplace proves. They believe it's impossible for people to not be influenced by their bias, another notion we strongly disagree with. "So," they ask, "why even try?" They argue that the only sensible approach is to work around bias, and they promote all kinds of tactics and systems to achieve it, such as blind hiring.

The term "blind hiring" goes back to the 1970s. Fearing lawsuits over discrimination against women, orchestras across the United States—which were almost completely composed of white, male musicians at that time—began auditioning musicians by having them play from behind a screen. And it worked. A study of eight major orchestras found that between 1970, when the blind auditions started, and 1993, when the study concluded, female membership in five top-ranked orchestras in the United States rose from 6 percent to 21 percent. The study credited blind auditions for a portion of that increase and the overall decline in gender-bias hiring.[34] That success caught the attention of the business world.

Today, blind hiring in corporations begins with scrubbing the resume. Advocates suggest removing names, schools, birthdates, or any other group-identifying elements. Some even champion eliminating resumes altogether and replacing them with skills tests or work samples. With the clean resumes or skills tests in hand, diverse selection teams are to conduct interviews using the same questions for all candidates and scoring their answers.

While all this looks virtuous on paper, it doesn't work in the real world. It can't. Especially for executive-level candidates. The talents and soft skills required of most managers and executives can't be evaluated well from a test, a few samples, or, frankly, from the other side of an opaque screen. And often when it comes to filling senior positions and board openings, those doing the hiring and promoting already know personally, or at least recognize, the candidates being considered. Even if their names are removed from their resumes, their projects and accomplishments reveal their identities.

But more to the point, no matter how "blind" the process, new hires are going to show up for work in the flesh one day, bringing their gender, race, age, background, cognitive preferences, and all the other characteristics that make them who they are with them. If the company has not been working to improve inclusion, all the issues of the Critical Mass Case will pop up.

There is one more practicality worth considering here: If you don't know candidates' backgrounds or unique traits during the interview process, how can you hire a diverse team?

MOTIVATION MUST COME FROM WITHIN

What all of this comes down to is that no matter how strong our case, DEI cannot reach its full potential through logic, peer pressure, or workarounds. Sure, we might be able to force diversity through numbers, but we can't force inclusion. You can't reward people into it, punish them into it, or order them into it. Extrinsic motivation simply isn't enough for human beings to overcome our baked-in tendencies to exclude those we perceive as different from us.

Yet, within every organization we've ever worked with, there are always several individuals who are attracted to diversity and inherently inclined to be inclusive. They don't need to be convinced of DEI's value or talked into to implementing DEI strategies. They are driven from within to work with different types of people, see them as individuals, and consider them part of their in-group.

That is the type of motivation needed to move DEI beyond bias and into the C-suite. But is it even possible to develop such a drive in another?

5

SELF-DETERMINED MOTIVATION

Motivation is the art of getting people to do what you want them to do because they want to do it.

—DWIGHT D. EISENHOWER

D rs. Edward Deci and Richard Ryan, psychologists at the University of Rochester, have been at the forefront of research into human motivation and personality for decades. Their findings, placed in a frame called "self-determination theory," view human motivation on a spectrum—from amotivation (the complete absence of motivation), to extrinsic motivation (being driven by external factors, such as rewards or penalties), to intrinsic motivation (acting for its own sake).[35]

INTRINSIC MOTIVATION

Intrinsically motivated people act from within. Their actions reflect who they are as people, independent of what others might expect or want. Their investment is in the experience and learning from it. Think of inventors who tinker in their shops. They don't do it for money or fame; they simply are driven to know how something works and whether it can work better. According to Deci and Ryan, the intrinsically motivated "have more interest, excitement, and confidence" than those who are motivated by outside factors, which results in "enhanced performance, persistence, and creativity."[36]

Intrinsic motivation produces the strongest and most powerful drive. And it's the level of motivation that people—especially those in leadership positions—must have to develop inclusion and equity in the workplace to mitigate their biases and reap the rewards of diversity.

NURTURING OUR NATURE

Self-determination theory posits that we're all born intrinsically motivated to reach toward the novel and get to know the world. After all, babies don't need to be bribed to bat at a mobile, open a kitchen cupboard, or figure out how to crawl. As we grow, however, our environment can tamp down that natural curiosity and drive.[37] Good behavior can become only about winning approval, learning merely a means to good grades, and work more about pay than passion. We can start to populate our in-groups with people who don't challenge our brains or worldviews.

While this common downward slide on self-determination theory's motivation spectrum may appear discouraging, self-determination theory argues that if our environment can have a negative effect on our motivation level, then it certainly can be designed to have a positive one.[38] So, although we can't force others or ourselves to be intrinsically motivated toward those who are different, we might be able to create workplace environments that encourage people to regain the intrinsic motivation they were born with.

SETTLERS, TRAVELERS, AND EXPLORERS

Before either of us knew anything about self-determination theory, the motivation spectrum, or intrinsic motivation, we developed and used a simpler scale to demonstrate to clients how different types of people react to DEI initiatives. It views a person's willingness (or lack thereof) to embrace the new and different through the lens of travel, placing people in one of three categories: settlers, travelers, or explorers.

Settlers, as the name implies, prefer to stay put. They see and experience all the world they're interested in from where they are. They prefer the people they've always known and doing things they've always done. Venturing beyond that familiar zone—meeting new people, trying new things— produces fear and anxiety in them.

When DEI initiatives ask settlers to form relationships outside their in-group, they aren't internally motivated to make the effort. But they aren't exactly unmotivated either; they're more nervous. Deep down, their inaction is not caused so much by a bias against particular out-group members—after all, they have no real experience with them specifically—but more by a bias against the unfamiliar in general and the need to keep that sense of unease at bay. By definition, it's a limiting state.

Travelers like to visit new places as long as they don't become too uncomfortable. They take in all the tourist sites, follow the recommended itineraries, and stay on the paved, well-lighted, more populated paths. They return home with some good stories and a few tchotchkes and settle back into their lives, fundamentally unchanged by their experience.

Travelers can and do participate in workplace DEI efforts. They understand DEI as a means to a specific end. They contentedly work beside those who are different, because it's good for business, it's morally right, or it's what's required to do the job. And so financial success, being seen as a good person, or a regular paycheck motivates them to achieve diversity. But since inclusiveness isn't necessary to that transaction, the motivation to achieve it isn't there for the traveler.

Explorers take off to new places without expectation of what they'll find. They venture off the beaten path and immerse themselves in new experiences—meeting the locals, eating the cuisine, and struggling with the language. Explorers love to plow new ground. They like to learn and see things through different eyes. They are comfortable being uncomfortable. They absorb new experiences and are changed by them.

Explorers welcome DEI into their workplaces. They see it as an opportunity to expand their circle and their knowledge. They are inclusive by nature because they never lost the intrinsic motivation they were born with.

THE INTRINSIC INCLUSION MINDSET

In our own travels, we've observed specific patterns of behavior that intrinsically inclusive individuals—typically explorers—consistently demonstrate, resulting in substantial benefits for the organizations they serve.

The five characteristics of people with an intrinsically inclusive mindset are:

1. They seek to build relationships with those who are like and unlike themselves with the same amount of enthusiasm. This includes relationships with other employees, customers, vendors, and consumer groups.

2. They have a natural curiosity to learn more about people who are unlike themselves. This means they go after, and thus gain a deeper understanding of, such things as customer/consumer markets, competitors, and potential new markets.

3. They have less unjustified fear and negative stereotyping of those who are different. Therefore, they often build highly effective, diverse, and inclusive teams.

4. They know that they might make mistakes in dealing with those who are different, but that doesn't deter them from pursuing relationships. They readily acknowledge and learn from a mistake and act to rectify the situation.

5. And they consistently deliver to their corporations the advantages of diversity, equity, and inclusion, e.g.,

increased employee engagement, innovation, better problem solving, lower turnover, and bottom-line benefits.

Self-determination theory does show us that everyone—no matter where they currently fall on the motivation spectrum—can recapture or at least move closer to the intrinsic motivation they were born with, so they can realize for themselves and their businesses DEI's many benefits.

According to self-determination theory, for intrinsic motivation to exist, three innate psychological needs must be met: relatedness, competence, and autonomy.[39]

- Relatedness happens when people are genuinely interested in taking an action: they want to do it. A person who feels a relatedness toward DEI would be authentically curious about other people, other cultures, and other ways of thinking about and solving problems. Such a person would seek out interactions and relationships with people who expand their knowledge rather than those who reinforce what they already know.

- Competence comes from people believing they have the skill set to meet the task. For DEI, that would mean confidence in the ability to relate to a wide variety of people—to not be frightened or repelled by differences.

- Autonomy occurs when people feel self-governed, completely unencumbered from outside influences in choosing actions and behaviors. For example, they aren't acting to meet goals or reacting to avoid lawsuits.

Until now, DEI efforts have fallen short in meeting these needs. Thanks to social psychology and social neuroscience, we now know that our brains aren't likely to be driven to relate to people who are different—quite the opposite. And when it comes to competence in engaging with out-group members, most people don't feel secure in their abilities. They're afraid they'll say the wrong thing, do the wrong thing, or make one mistake and lose their job. As for autonomy in DEI, corporations typically haven't encouraged it. Rather than ask or guide, they tell their people that they need to build diverse teams and be champions of DEI. Justifiably, they are trying to build more diversity into their cultures, but they are doing it through an extrinsic push.

Therefore, when you look at all three legs of the self-determination theory stool in corporations today, not one leg stands firm. Thankfully, this is because we didn't know better. And now we do.

Deci and Ryan write that intrinsic motivation is heightened by "choice, acknowledgment of feelings, and opportunities for self-direction," while "tangible rewards," as well as "threats, deadlines, directives, pressured evaluations, and imposed goals diminish intrinsic motivation."[40] As we work to strengthen each leg of the self-determination theory stool and construct a workplace environment that encourages intrinsic inclusion, we must identify, rethink, and replace practices that negate or discourage them. And we must create strategies, policies, and learning opportunities that serve to satisfy, enhance, and support them.

6

BREAKTHROUGH

Working With Our Wiring

Do the best you can until you know better.
Then, when you know better, do better.

—MAYA ANGELOU

Creating a workplace environment conducive to intrinsic motivation and the explorer's mindset starts with understanding the environment in our heads. Just as social psychology and social neuroscience have shown us that implicit biases (preconceived attitudes) often dictate our judgments and behaviors without our realizing it, both disciplines also show us how to work with our rebooted brain's wiring to pause these automatically activated attitudes when we want to, open up our thought processes, and base our judgments and behaviors on reality.

THE MIND OF THE BEHOLDER

Our perceptions are constructive in nature. What we bring to a situation—our memories, our ambitions, our attitudes, and our stereotypes (implicit bias's fuel)—are as important, if not more important, in determining our thoughts about something than the actual physical stimuli.

For instance, an approaching dog (physical stimulus) immediately delights one person, frightens another, and registers as nothing more than a dog to someone else. As the dog gets closer, it begins wagging its tail. The person who likes dogs interprets this action as positive and moves toward the dog to pet it. The person who doesn't like dogs is suspicious of the tail and moves to avoid the animal. The third person reads nothing into the dog's actions and so doesn't change their behavior at all. All three people see the same animal yet perceive it differently.

Dr. Fazio might note here that the activation of the attitude is what's implicit (unrealized), not the attitude itself, meaning that these three people are well aware of, and responsible for, how they feel about dogs. What they don't realize is how that attitude is solely defining their judgment about, and behavior toward, this particular dog, which they have not experienced and know nothing about.

Basing a judgment—and probably action—on old information that may or may not have any validity in the current situation has one set of consequences when you're talking about a dog and quite another when you're trying to decide whom to hire or whose idea to explore or which project to invest in.

This finding caused Dr. Fazio of The Ohio State University and Dr. Michael Olson of the University of Tennessee to pose the question: As our neurons make their way from stimuli to perception, is there a way to prevent those preconceptions from hijacking our thoughts and determining our judgment? [41]

MODE: CLEARING THE WAY FOR INTRINSIC MOTIVATION

The answer they found was "Yes," it is possible to put the brakes on implicit bias. Specifically, they found that "motivation and opportunity can be determinants of spontaneous behavior"—a theory known as the MODE model.[42] Dr. Fazio often refers to MODE as a "gating mechanism." With enough motivation and the opportunity, our brains can shut the gate on or interrupt an automatically activated attitude and allow new information to enter the thought process, resulting in deliberate, better informed decisions and actions.

Motivation can be defined as any incentive that causes a person to stop and think about outcomes—such as concern for safety, sticking to a budget, avoiding embarrassment, or important new information. Opportunity can be defined as "people having the resources" to think clearly and consciously, meaning they aren't tired, in a hurry, or distressed.

MANUFACTURING MODE MOTIVATION

Perhaps, in some cases, we wonder if pausing the thought process requires the motivation to be as intense as the bias, which is a tall order when it comes to attitudes as ingrained and instinctual as those linked to DEI. But sharing a significant emotional event with "the other," frequent exposure to "the other" combined with significant relationships, or "syncing" (physically feeling what "the other" feels and through that, gaining empathy for them) can each engender the necessary level of motivation for our brains to open the gate to DEI. None of these motivators may depend on a rational argument or a tangible, measurable reward—they may all be tied to emotion.

REBOOT: A SIGNIFICANT EMOTIONAL EVENT

Imagine rushing your sick child to the hospital. A female doctor with a foreign accent instructs the nurses to get the child into an examining room "stat." In quick order, she relieves your child's (and your) distress. Within half an hour, your child is sitting up and laughing. Your worst fears allayed, you're overjoyed. Chances are, at this point, any biases against female, foreign doctors you walked into the ER with have been replaced by intense feelings of relief and gratitude. In fact, your brain likely has started to assign her—and all female, foreign doctors—in-group traits such as competence and trustworthiness.

Significant emotional events such as this may upend patterned thinking. We experience a new reality and new possibilities, which may cause new neural connections and pathways to form. The next time a similar stimulus activates the old attitude, and our neurons start to take off toward an old judgment, they find themselves at a crossroads. That pause is all our brains need to consider new information and stop the implicit bias.

This level of motivation in the workplace—especially with executives—usually derives from a very personal event. For instance, male executives are likely to re-examine their own attitudes toward gender discrimination after a daughter has been a victim of it. Executives nearing retirement age often stop discounting older workers. And painful discrimination lawsuits often motivate leadership teams to be more attentive to DEI throughout their organizations.

REBOOT: FREQUENT EXPOSURE + SIGNIFICANT RELATIONSHIPS

Exposure alone does not eradicate bias, but it can weaken it enough to let a few significant relationships form that will cause the brain to pause, so it can question old attitudes.

Let's say you're at a pretty average height for an American adult. And of course, having grown up in the United States, most other adults you know are more than five feet tall, and many are more than six feet tall.

Then, you're sent on assignment to a village where the majority of fully grown adults are around four feet in height. It's a little disconcerting at first. After all, in your mind's eye, you see an adult—and all traits of competence and responsibility attached to that word—as someone with at least another twelve or so inches on them. While you wouldn't say you are biased against shorter people—in fact, you've never consciously thought about it—you do understandably regard being taller as preferable.

After a few weeks in the village, your brain experiences a reset of sorts. Through sustained exposure, you no longer react to the villagers' height; your brain accepts (because you have experienced) that perfectly competent adults can be four feet tall. However, given a choice between a villager who's four feet tall and someone who is six feet tall, your brain is still likely to default toward a preference for the taller person.

To produce motivation strong enough to defeat that bias and allow you to see and judge individuals for who they are— not their height—your frequent exposure needs a push from a significant relationship or two. As you form friendships with a few villagers and bond over what you do have in common, new neural pathways may form, along with emotional connectivity. Your brain categorizes these new friends as your in-group and so regards others with similar traits positively until proven otherwise. Old biases fade away. Your thoughts about four-foot-tall adults become based in reality, unswayed by bias, upping the quality of your opinion, your thoughts, and their outcomes.

Now, just for fun, pretend your next assignment is to an island where the average adult is seven feet tall. All of a sudden, you're the short one. You embody the very trait you've been biased against. Your feet don't touch the floor when you sit in their chairs, you have trouble reaching shelves, and you must look up at people to communicate. Your height, which always seemed just right to you, now seems inadequate. You find yourself being self-conscious and defensive. Afraid of being judged negatively, stereotype threat creeps in and begins affecting what you think and how you behave.

When you finally return home and surround yourself with other adults you can look in the eye, you realize that your journeys into the lands of the short and the tall have provided you with an entirely new attitude—or lack of attitude—toward height. Height has been shown to you to be just a number—not a referendum on smarts or competence. You laugh at yourself for ever having considered yourself superior or inferior for a trait you had nothing to do with and no control over. You dispelled your attitudes toward body size.

Of course, these lands are imaginary. But still, they illustrate why travel or similar types of exposure can be so great in combatting bias and encouraging inclusion. It gets us out of what we've always known and opens our minds to different experiences and ways of doing things.

REBOOT: "SYNCING"

Dr. Andrea Serino is a leader in the study of peri-personal space. As head of neuroscience at MindMaze and invited professor at the Center for Neuroprosthetics of École Polytechnique Federale de Lausanne (Swiss Federal Institute of Technology), he and his research team, often using virtual reality, examine how our brains create our experience of our bodies, including our peri-personal space (the space between us and those we are relating to). They seek to understand how we feel our body and how we use our sense of body to interact with others.

One of those ways is through "syncing" (our term), which occurs when our brains integrate another's physical experience with our experience of ourselves. This phenomenon is shown in research conducted by Dr. Serino. When we physically move with another person or watch another person receive physical stimuli, we can actually begin to feel in our own bodies what the other person feels in theirs. As we "sync up," we may also gain empathy toward the other person (feeling them to be our own selves), reducing and even eliminating negative biases.

Dr. Serino explained to us that synchronized movement is where our senses of trust and belonging as human beings originate. As infants, we're held and rocked by our parents and caretakers. We are soothed by the rhythms of their heartbeats. We find safety in their arms and are given sustenance as we move together. All of this manifests as a physical trigger deep in our brains. Throughout our lives, rhythmic movement may continue to set off that sense of trust and belonging we knew as babies—and the feel-good body chemistry that goes with it.

Without consciously understanding all that, we may use this trigger all the time in our everyday lives to build connection and bond with other people. It's why soldiers march, couples dance, churchgoers sing, and sports fans cheer together—"syncing."

I FEEL YOU—LITERALLY

Dr. Serino explained to us: "Our brains generate this experience (of the body) by integrating multi-sensory stimuli coming from the body. I know my hand is my hand because I receive coherent signals from it: I see my hand moving. I touch something, and I get tactile feedback. If I send a motor command to my hand, it moves." That multi-sensory stimuli—such as touching, feeling, moving—set off a very specific set of neurons in our brains that gives us our sense of physical self.

Amazingly, that same set of neurons can be sparked when we watch someone else (in person or virtually) being touched—an occurrence Dr. Serino calls "visual remapping of touch" (VRT). We feel what the other person feels.[43] Perhaps that may lead to emotional connection and empathy.

Not surprisingly, the more the other person looks like us, the more easily and more intensely we feel what they feel. This same ease and escalation in feeling can also occur due to shared values—such as political beliefs.[44] Though it takes a little more effort without shared traits or known shared values, "syncing" may still have the ability to form strong bonds among people and the motivation needed to pause a bias.

CHECKING YOUR EMPATHY

All three of these motivation builders (reboots)—the significant emotional event, frequent exposure combined with significant relationships, and "syncing"—are built on the premise of connection and empathy. When you feel what another human being feels, and you see them for who they are, it's hard to judge them with an old bias. Yet, not all types of empathy—yes, there are types of empathy—produce such revelations. Some actually add fuel to implicit bias, extinguishing motivation.

At our Neuroscience of Diversity and Inclusion Workshop, Dr. Steven Spencer explained an experiment where he and his team asked white, European-American subjects to imagine three different scenarios in a day in the life of Tyrone Williams, an African American student. As we recall the dialogue with Dr. Spencer, the first group was to imagine Tyrone arguing with his professor about a grade he thought was unfair.

They were told to take Tyrone's perspective, imagine themselves doing the arguing, and then consider how such a task would take strength and build character. The second group was told again to imagine Tyrone confronting his professor about a grade. But this time, they were to think about how difficult the task would be for him and the confrontation he'd likely face. In the control scenario, subjects were to think about Tyrone going through a day doing routine tasks.

The first scenario created what Dr. Spencer calls respectful empathy. The subjects in this group felt admiration for Tyrone and his ability to overcome a challenge, and their "perceptions of competence" toward Tyrone increased.

The second group generated what Dr. Spencer calls a paternalistic empathy toward Tyrone, meaning empathy plus concern. While they, too, felt for him, what they felt was pity, which decreased their perceptions of competence in him. Dr. Spencer explained that paternalistic empathy creates problems because you don't see the other person for what they can contribute or what they can bring to the interaction. You just say, "Aw, poor you." And that sort of reaction isn't helpful.

According to Dr. Spencer, in our minds, paternalistic empathy increases the power differential between ourselves and those toward whom we have empathy. We not only feel we're stronger—and so better than, making them less than in our minds—we also pat ourselves on the back for these feelings. All of this causes our thought processes to backfire and go for the stereotype, bolstering our automatically activated attitudes. Respectful empathy, on the other hand, helps us regard the other person as an individual and adds to our esteem for them, discounting old biases and stereotypes and adding to our motivation to be inclusive.

BEWARE OF EMPATHY BLOCKERS

When it comes to the quality of our empathy, there's more to consider than just our heads and thought processes. According to our recollection of a conversation with Dr. Baldwin Way, there is increasing evidence that when our immune system is activated, our amygdalas show the same heightened response as when they detect a social threat (an angry face or social rejection). Imagine if somebody is suffering economic stress—they've lost their job or there's a recession—and they see somebody from an out-group; there might be a lot of psychological processing.

The effect of heightened or sustained stress might truly be an empathy blocker. This is especially important to consider in our current business environments where multitasking, rapid decision-making, and uncertainty are the norm.

GUARANTEEING THE OPPORTUNITY

Even the strongest motivation requires the "opportunity" to do its job and disrupt our implicit biases. As Dr. Fazio explains, implicit bias is more likely to affect our judgment when "we're tired, in a bad mood, or under a time pressure." Although the motivation is there, our brains don't have the energy to pause the automatically activated attitude already in progress. "When the workload is high, people are going to rely on shortcuts and associative clues," he warns.[45]

Therefore, providing the opportunity for MODE and gaining control over our thought processes comes down to being aware of stressors and removing them when possible. While we can't regulate people's moods or life events, we can educate leadership and staff as to how deadlines, hunger, exhaustion, stereotype threat, out-group threat, and the like can affect their ability to make a bias-free decision. We can put systems in place and establish best practices to ensure that when people make important decisions and take consequential actions, their brains are rested, nourished, and calm, and they've checked their bias.

FROM IMPLICIT BIAS TO INTRINSIC INCLUSION

MODE shows us that we are not prisoners of implicit or unconscious bias—or any bias, for that matter. We don't have to be stuck in our ways, as they say. We now know that we can use our brains to reveal our biases, hold them up to the light, and change those that limit us. Through awareness and working with our brains' wiring (not pushing against it), we can put ourselves, our goals, and reality back in charge of our thought processes and our lives. "The more you find yourself checking your attitude," Dr. Fazio says, "the more the attitude weakens and can be replaced with a new association."[46] Remember, our attitudes are nothing more than memories of past experiences. The more experiences we allow ourselves to have, the more information our brains have to go on, and the more our limiting biases are likely to disintegrate as our thinking evolves.

With the right environment in place—supported by brain-based DEI learning experiences, systems, policies, and practices—intrinsic motivation and an explorer's mindset can regain their positions in our thought processes and move our default from implicit bias to intrinsic inclusion.

7

FIELD TESTING

Creating an Ideal DEI Environment

*Given that we face no shortage of
difficult and complex problems, we have
little choice but to leverage our differences.*

—SCOTT PAGE, *The Difference*[47]

E arly in our careers, we worked with the CEO of a small, community hospital. Former military, he was an effective, no-excuses kind of manager. Within a very short tenure, he had improved the hospital's performance considerably and shored up its financials. His next step, and why he hired our firm, was to embed diversity, equity, and inclusion into everyday operations. On paper, this leader understood the benefits of DEI, especially to a healthcare institution. Even then, there were plenty of studies demonstrating how bias impedes a provider's ability to diagnose and prescribe, negatively affecting patient outcomes.

Although he was gung-ho about the idea of DEI, he himself had trouble integrating its concepts into his own work and decision-making. To his straitlaced, by-the-book mind, a circumstance was a circumstance; a fact, a fact—who perceived it or how they perceived it shouldn't matter. To him (as is the case with most of us until we become aware), his thought processes and choices were rational and right. How could designing an insurance form or deciding on how much security to hire contain bias? But, as science now tells us, without pausing to consider our biases, our brains are going to opt for the ease and efficiency of automatically activated attitudes, guaranteeing that we miss opportunities for inclusion, even when designing something as seemingly straightforward as an insurance form.

Of course, at that time, we as consultants didn't have neuroscience to guide us. But we did have plenty of field evidence that providing experiences for clients helped them understand the importance of diversity and inclusion better than words ever could. Simulated exercises were always a big part of our efforts.

We had this CEO and his leadership team navigate the hospital as patients. Some of the executives were blindfolded. Some were given crutches. Some were put on gurneys, so they could view the patient experience from that vulnerable angle. The CEO was put in a wheelchair in the parking lot and told to make his way to the admitting desk.

With all confidence, he wheeled himself from a handicapped parking spot up to the sidewalk and started up the ramp that had been newly installed to code and on his approval. As he made his way, this physically fit man with huge, powerful arms began to struggle. He stopped well before he reached the automatic doors, breathing heavily, "Wow." he said, "I never took into account the length of this ramp. I didn't realize or think about people who might not have someone to push their chair or help them. It's a long way from the parking lot. We need to do something different here. This isn't serving our patients." Then he took that thought even further. "I've always thought every patient who came to this hospital was greeted with the same respect and had the same opportunity for care. And here I sit—I can't even make it to the door to be greeted."

Something clicked for him that day, and he was finally able to internalize—to understand from the inside out, intrinsically—what incorporating diversity, equity, and inclusion can mean for an organization, and the missed opportunities that result from discounting it. In the environment we created for him, this CEO was able to pause his old attitude. And because he was educated on diversity, equity, and inclusion, he knew to fill that pause with actual experience and redirect his thought processes.

The result was transformational for him, for his staff, and for the hospital and its patients. From that day forward, his brain defaulted to an explorer's mindset; he'd become intrinsically inclusive (though we didn't know that term yet either). He asked questions, gathered different points of view, and weighed various outcomes before determining the best solution. His new approach was contagious and organically produced an environment that both modeled and fostered inclusion in his increasingly diverse staff— producing the engagement, innovation, and empowerment that come with it.

That CEO has long since retired. And his hospital (like most small hospitals) has been acquired several times. But to this day, its hallways remain adorned with art he chose. It's an eclectic collection of local works that remind all who walk by of the diversity of the community the hospital serves, and the deep well of perspectives, creativity, and resources that springs from it.

Today, DEI professionals no longer need to work in the dark, relying solely on field observations for what works for organizations and what doesn't. We can use (and are using) scientific theory to create environments that help both leadership and staff develop an explorer's mindset, meet the psychological needs for intrinsic motivation, and take their workplaces from transactional to transformational. Based on what we now know, in order to become intrinsically inclusive, our brains need the desire for DEI; an understanding of bias and how it works; and an environment that can help us to slow our thought processes down, monitor our assumptions, and remove perceived threats. The desire and understanding can be achieved through education and by changing the workplace environment through tweaks in our current systems, practices, and procedures.

Of course, even in the best environment, not everyone will take on a full-blown explorer's mindset and achieve intrinsic inclusion. But everyone will move that much closer to them. And that will move DEI forward faster—and eventually into the C-suite.

BIAS BUY-IN

The foundational building block for the ideal DEI environment is the acceptance of bias. To be able to advance DEI in an organization, everyone must accept and be comfortable with the fact that they have biases, and that those biases are present, sometimes without their awareness, in every decision they make.

This used to be a tough sell. People often equate bias with prejudice. They are understandably resistant to the idea that they are "prejudiced," with all the negative connotations society assigns to that. They also reject the notion that they don't control their thoughts and that their judgment is often usurped by attitudes they weren't completely aware they had.

Introducing bias, unconscious bias, and implicit bias from a scientific point of view, however, can make both of those facts much easier for everyone to accept. It takes the emotion out of it. And it shows bias for what it is—a universal, shared trait among all human beings to be discussed and dealt with as a fact and a feature of our brains, not a personal failing.

One frequently used, objective tool in this endeavor can be the Implicit Association Test (IAT). Developed by Project Implicit, a nonprofit international collaboration among researchers, the IAT allows people to discover and explore their own implicit biases. This is a series of tests developed by Dr. Mahzarin Banaji, where people can choose to uncover their attitudes in the areas of weight, weapons, age, Arab-Muslims, race, religion, disability, sexuality, skin-tone, presidents, transgenderism, Asian Americans, gender and science, gender and career, and Native Americans. The IAT is free and available online. (More detailed information on Project Implicit and a link to the tests can be found in the notes on our website: www.intrinsicinclusion.com.) One professional we knew, who had always struggled with weight and so was mindful not to judge people's physical appearances, was dumbfounded when the test revealed that she maintained a preference for more slender people. According to Project Implicit's own data, an implicit bias toward societal norms isn't uncommon. People in "stigmatized" groups often regard others in their group in a positive light, yet they still maintain a "moderate preference" for those in the more "socially valued" group.[48] As we attempt to open our minds, our workplaces, and our world to diverse people and ideas, this is useful information to have about ourselves.

Once bias and implicit bias are acknowledged, we can work with them.

BUILD MODE INTO THE ROUTINE

The MODE theory gives us a methodology for putting a stop to our implicit bias and regaining control over our thought processes and their outcomes. But as we know, slowing down our thought processes long enough to stop our automatically activated attitudes is more easily said than done—even when we are highly motivated. Therefore, it makes sense to install practices into our routines to cause that pause, giving our brains time to consider our biases and add some new infor-mation to our thought processes if we wish.

A few such tactics that have proven successful in doing that and can easily be integrated into an organization's decision-making processes are:

1. Flip the Script

   Say you decide someone is performing poorly and so should not be promoted. As a way to ensure that implicit bias is not playing a role in that judgment, Dr. Fazio recommends "flipping the script"—meaning consider the opposite. In this instance, it would mean entertaining the scenario that the person has performed well and should be promoted, and then searching your brain for evidence to support that thought. Dr. Fazio suggested to us that this extra effort provides the pause necessary to interrupt and challenge an implicit bias. It also nudges people into an explorer's mindset—looking at something or someone from a different angle.[49]

   Flipping of the script can be prompted by something as simple as a one-page decision-making tool that lays out the process in checklist form and reminds people to do it.

2. Say It Out Loud

   Again, Dr. Fazio explained to us that when people justify their decisions out loud to someone else, they are likely to correct for bias. Having to put thoughts into words obviously slows down the thought process. It also forces us to think more completely and logically. What might make perfect sense in our heads often sounds ridiculous coming out of our mouths.

   "Saying it out loud" can become part of a company's culture. Before any consequential decision is decreed—such as whom to hire, fire, or promote, or whose project to invest in—executives must explain their decision and their reasoning out loud to a peer or group of peers. Whether the process confirms a decision or negates it, any bias can be checked.

3. De-stress Decisions

As we've learned, stress, hunger, and exhaustion open the floodgates to implicit bias. The strained brain takes the path of least resistance; it doesn't have the energy to forge new neural pathways. While we can't change our biology, we can put practices in place that guard against making big decisions when our brains are tired or lacking fuel.

For instance, we might make it policy that interviews and major meetings are to be held in the morning—when the majority of people are most alert. We could also create lists for checking our mindsets before heading into those interviews or meetings. That list might include reminders such as: we've allotted enough time for our task, we are not overscheduled, we're well rested, we've eaten and are hydrated, we are satisfied with our research and the information we have, and we are prepared to consider the opposite.

Building MODE's pauses into our everyday work routines ensures that everyone's thought processes have the time and the awareness they need to make the best, most informed, least automatic decisions possible. It makes biases easier to catch or, at the very least, check—giving the control (autonomy) back to the decision makers, causing them to feel more confidence in their decision (competence). Diversity, equity, and inclusion get the room and consideration needed to take root in an organization's culture and grow.

MIND YOUR MEASURES

The metrics used in the workplace to evaluate and make judgments about people and their potential—test scores, deals closed, class rank, profits made, number of projects worked on—can seem like neutral measures. At first glance, they look like fair gauges of a person's past performance. But that's rarely reality.

Let's say you had a salesperson who hit their quarterly target—100 percent. And you had another who made only 95 percent of their target in the same quarter. Based on the metrics alone, you might conclude that the first salesperson was better at sales, had more potential, and should be promoted. But digging a little deeper, you find that the second salesperson reached 95 percent though their territory had suffered a hurricane that shut down businesses for a month during the quarter. Who is the better salesperson now? Who has more potential?

Context matters. And numbers rarely provide context.

Unless we've been alerted otherwise, our brains tend to assume that everyone starts at the same place with the same number of obstacles and amount of support. By definition, with a diverse workforce that's never true. In a 2013 study, Dr. Spencer and his colleagues found that "common measures of academic performance systemically understate the intellectual ability and potential of members of negatively stereotyped groups."[50]

As an example, Dr. Spencer explained to us that grade point averages (GPAs) or test scores provide limited information. He pointed out, for instance, that a 3.7 GPA produced by a student who works a full-time job and manages food and housing insecurities might in reality be superior to a 4.0 GPA from a full-time student with no economic stressors. Yet, unless applications ask for such context, admissions officers may never receive that information to consider.[51]

A workplace environment that supports intrinsic inclusion keeps our brains alert to context and nuance when it comes to judging the potential of others. An organization's merit systems must be evaluated for both bias and the absence of context before being accepted and used as a standard.

According to Dr. Spencer, it's relatively easy to spot where biased measures are being employed. Just look at where homogeneity reigns in your organization. You might have done a great job attracting both men and women of different races to your staff. But on closer examination, perhaps you see they're all between twenty-five and thirty-five years of age. That tells you that your hiring metrics may be skewed against older workers and that your company is missing their input. Or perhaps during a department meeting, you notice that everyone at the table has a spreadsheet in front of them. You might want to see whether your metric for staffing that department is too generous to analytical thinkers and biased against creatives.

To discourage biased measures and to give decision-makers more complete information to work with, Dr. Spencer suggests putting systems in place that 1) put all measures in context, 2) check for stereotype threat in evaluations, 3) broaden whatever measures the company does employ, and 4) when possible, gather input from a diverse set of evaluators.[52]

No metric can ever be perfectly fair and unbiased, but simply having a system of checks for measures in place can keep us aware and attuned to their hidden biases.

EXPAND EVERYONE'S IN-GROUP

Our brains are quick to assign in-group and out-group status—we've seen that it takes little more than the color of a sports jersey for us to start allocating positive or negative traits to people we don't even know. While we now know that these designations yield strong, emotion-filled, automatic attitudes, we also know that they are easily changed. Often it takes nothing more than finding out that we have one thing in common with an out-group member for our brains to switch their status to in-group.

The ideal DEI environment uses this brain quirk to its advantage. Through design and simple practices integrated into work routines, we can create environments that expand everyone's in-group and thereby reduce out-group threat and make inclusion happen.

We can start with something as basic as looking at how people physically move about the workplace. The ideal DEI environment promotes interaction among diverse populations on every floor and between floors. That allows for casual conversations that can result in people finding commonalities. All it takes is one shared interest for mere belonging to start yoking people together and allowing empathy to grow.

Executive floors, especially, may experience hurdles there, however. Having these segregated floors—which are usually incredibly homogeneous to begin with—prevents senior executives from passing by, interacting with, and even seeing people who are different from them and their peers. Because they don't have the opportunity to regularly experience a diverse population at work, diversity never truly gets normalized in their brains. When thinking through how spaces might be used to encourage interaction and mere belonging, pay special attention to leadership spaces, and ensure that they receive the same opportunities as the rest of the building for random engagement and thus bonding.

But a supportive DEI environment doesn't leave yoking to chance encounters alone. It also installs routine actions to enhance belonging:

- Ice breakers at the start of meetings can allow people to share some appropriate personal information—a favorite book or movie, the fact that they're caring for an elderly parent, or that they love anime. Such details allow people to see each other as individuals, not stereotypes.

- A common cause—whether work-related or a community project—puts everyone on the same team and that puts them in the same in-group. Ensure that the cause is well defined and that everyone knows they are pulling in the same direction for the same outcome.

- Regular events both on- and off-site can provide a needed but casual opportunity for team members with diverse backgrounds and talents to get together and get to know each other through shared experiences. Of course, be considerate of diverse lifestyles and disabilities when choosing activities. For instance, meeting at a bar after work for drinks with no variation excludes team members who have family responsibilities or people who may not be comfortable around alcohol.

Remember: experiences create new memories, and new memories form new attitudes.

Providing opportunities that encourage staff members to mingle with people they otherwise would never get to know also helps them to satisfy self-determination theory's three basic psychological needs for intrinsic motivation. Through mere belonging, people build up "relatedness"; through regular interaction, they gain "competence" in their ability to form relationships with people they perceive as different; and because these relationships are not assigned, they have the feeling of "autonomy" in forming them. As their familiarity with each other increases, so does their sense of belonging—and with that comes new neural pathways that enable changes in thoughts and behaviors, while increasing trust and engagement.

MOVE TOGETHER

Some of these social events might include activities that get people moving in sync, allowing them to further build empathy and trust. This doesn't take a ropes course or white-water rafting. Multi-sensory motor syncing can occur with activities that are inclusive of all body types and fitness levels, such as singing and swaying to music together.

In fact, we recently devised an exercise using the concept of syncing to promote trust and better understanding between executives. It requires only a stick—actually a cylindrical rod we call the "Syncing Stick." The rod is red on both ends and green in the middle. Each person holds an end, and then both are prompted into a meaningful conversation. For instance, we might ask them to start talking about what trust means or how they know when people are trustworthy.

As they talk, they, of course, move a bit, at least from one foot to the other. Through the Syncing Stick, they feel the other's movements. After a little time, they start to shift their weight together—in sync. Our experience so far has been that as they continue to interface and talk more deeply, their hands start to move closer to the middle of the stick—into the green zone—which we call the "Zone of Trust."

Although this is a brand-new exercise we've only had in the field for a year or so and done no formal research on, what our clients are reporting and what we are seeing is that people do end the exercise better able to hear and understand the other. It's simple and elegant, and so far, it's been successful.

UPEND STEREOTYPING

Not so long ago, we were facilitating a leadership session on diversity, equity, and inclusion. About thirty executives were present and seated at five breakout tables with six people each. Out of the thirty leaders, six were women.

"Okay," Vincent said, getting everyone geared up for the next exercise. "You're going to need two volunteers from your table: a scribe and a facilitator."

We watched them volunteer for the jobs. When all was said and done, all the facilitators were men, and four of the five scribes were women.

We stopped the exercise right there.

"Please," Vincent said. "I'd like all the scribes to stand up." And they all stood up—four women and one man.

Vincent continued, "What do you all see?" Everyone just stared. Vincent pointed out, "Almost unanimously, you chose men to lead the exercise and women to record it."

"Oh well," one man said, "I don't have good handwriting. I don't spell so well." The others nodded in agreement.

"But everyone in here is a corporate leader," Vincent reminded them. "Are you telling me that most of you can't spell well enough to take notes?"

Then a few of the women came to the men's defense. "Oh," they said. "I volunteered because I really don't mind being the scribe."

"And I'm glad you volunteered, because I asked for volunteers," Vincent said. "However, don't you think it's worth a conversation that even though there are only six women here, they are the majority of scribes? Where did that come from? Why is that okay?"

While it may not be okay, it's typical. As this exercise shows, the men weren't forcing the women to scribe—the women volunteered for it and deferred to the men when it came to the leadership role, even defending them. And these were executives attending a diversity, equity, and inclusion leadership session. You can imagine how insidious stereotyping is in less-aware surroundings.

Stereotyping is the antithesis of intrinsic inclusion. It puts people in a box they can't get out of. Creating an environment that makes people notice and then challenge stereotypes is imperative to moving closer to intrinsic inclusion becoming the brain's default setting.

To open minds, broaden opportunities, and squash stereotypes, every interview process, every vendor-selection process, every promotion process, and every process that deals with selecting people for a role should include a "should look like" check. Before the selection process begins, people should be reminded to ask themselves, "What does a (fill in the blank) look like? What does a security guard look like? A nurse? A human-resources person? A customer?

An executive vice president for sales? A CEO?" Then, they conjure their stereotype in their mind's eye and recognize their bias—maybe even say it out loud. Next, they actively picture a person or several different people in that role who don't fit their stereotype. This exercise ensures that everyone enters the selection process fully aware of their bias and having made some new neural connections to open their minds beyond the stereotype.

NOTE AND USE COGNITIVE PREFERENCES

Just like people come in different shapes and sizes from a wide variety of cultural backgrounds, each with their own unique talents, they all also come with different preferences in how they think, learn, make decisions, and interact with others. For instance, some people rely heavily on facts and figures. Others go with their gut and make decisions based on how they feel. Some people are intuitive by nature. Others are more free-thinking and relational. Some people think in absolutes, some in concepts.

Being aware of and appreciating our cognitive diversity can ease tensions and improve communications. Thus, it's useful in building empathy, which leads to trust, feelings of belonging, and thus inclusion.

Say someone who is detail-oriented is assigned to work on a project with someone who is a big-picture thinker. If they aren't aware of their own thinking preferences or their partner's, working together is likely to be a struggle and unpleasant. The detail person might regard the big-picture person as unrealistic and lazy. The big-picture person might see the detail person as uncreative, negative, and nitpicking.

And both likely don't even recognize the blind spots in their own thinking.

But if they enter their partnership with full awareness of their own and each other's thinking styles, they can lean on one another's strengths, make up for each other's weaknesses, and form a strong partnership. Leveraging these differences results in a better project or solution and a better relationship than they otherwise would have had.

Herrmann, a transformative thinking company, offers a tool—the Herrmann Brain Dominance Instrument (HBDI®), which identifies preferences in thinking and processing information. Once preferences are identified and charted, then their Herrmann Whole Brain® Model guides you in putting what you learn to work.

The company's founder, the late Ned Herrmann, began developing his Whole Brain theory in the 1980s while head of management education at General Electric's world-class corporate university at Crotonville. Today highly validated, both the Herrmann assessment and the model are used by corporations and firms—including ours—throughout the world to strengthen team communication, problem-solving, and outcomes. (You can find out more about HBDI and the Herrmann Whole Brain Model in the notes on our website: www.intrinsicinclusion.com.) Like bias, bringing a curious awareness to our cognitive diversity takes the judgment and emotional charge out of it. Once you know that John in human resources is a relational thinker, you are less likely to be annoyed when he hands you the office birthday card to sign. You now understand that's just how he thinks. And the next time you're at a networking event, you also know to appreciate and leverage his people skills.

LEVERAGE THAT BIAS: DIVERGENT COLLABORATION

As we learned through implicit bias, our perceptions are constructive, made out of our experiences and memories. And because no two people have the same experiences or memories or exact cognitive preferences, everybody sees things differently, and so everybody has a unique point of view—or you could say "bias"—to contribute. Thus, the ideal DEI environment doesn't shy away from bias. It acknowledges it, is aware of it, and, whenever possible, puts it to good use to expand the organization's thinking and choices.

Advisory groups with diverse membership should be established to help with big decisions—such as overall company direction, human resource policies, and customer experience. In such an environment, people feel safe to weigh in with their opinions, reducing stereotype threat. They also become used to paying attention to their biases, so they don't become implicit. And they are regularly exposed to a variety of points of view—promoting an explorer's mindset all around.

Taking this leveraging of diversity even further, Dr. Bart Barthelemy, director of the IDEA Lab at the Wright Brothers Institute, explained a new approach to problem solving to us that was developed and applied in their lab. It's called Divergent Collaboration.[SM] The process takes the phrase "out of the box" to a whole new level. And Dr. Barthelemy recommends its use for mostly new and more complex challenges.

Instead of using people with direct and thorough knowledge of the issue or challenge, Divergent Collaboration brings together individuals who have knowledge that's not directly applicable to the problem but is tangential to it.

If our problem is determining how to get people to be intrinsically inclusive, we don't gather a group solely of DEI professionals and psychologists who specialize in inclusion. We form a group that might include a person in a biracial marriage, a judge who is used to hearing two sides of a story, a hypnotist who knows that thoughts below the surface motivate behavior, an FBI agent who can read people's motives, and others until we have a group of about fifteen people from different walks of life with different perspectives.

The person who has the challenge (the challenge owner) is brought in to explain the issue but doesn't weigh in on a solution or give direction. The group then splits up into teams. They restate the problem through their various lenses and start talking. Then the challenge owner returns and listens to what they have to say. The challenge owner then combines these fresh, different ideas with what they know to be possible, to form a solution.

The process results in exposing avenues of thoughts and solutions that a more traditional problem-solving team would not have the experience or knowledge to even imagine. However, Dr. Barthelemy cautions, Divergent Collaboration is only useful to teams that are willing to keep an open mind, to be fearless about what's possible, and to consider untraditional routes and solutions.

Besides being a fascinating approach to problem solving, Divergent Collaboration is also a beautiful example of the power of diversity, equity, and inclusion to drive innovation. People from multiple disciplines are aligned around a particular problem. The fact of their diversity opens the challenge up and allows the experts to see new angles, new facets, new directions—and to find new solutions that couldn't have been revealed any other way.

AN EXPLORER'S ENVIRONMENT

In our own education programs, we often facilitate an exercise we call "Uniquely Me/Uniquely You." We start with a list of about fifty random traits—including female, male, served in the military, over fifty, under forty, can make beef stroganoff, has traveled to Europe—as we said, random. As we read each trait, people who identify with that trait stand. As people pop out of their chairs, they spontaneously smile at each other in shared recognition; some high-five. Laughter always breaks out. They've found, and they feel, a connection.

Next, we ask them to characterize themselves as individuals by listing ten things that make them who they are. Then we ask them to find someone in the room they don't know, and share their list. And that person, in turn, shares their list.

Now these pairs usually find that they have some things in common, and they have differences as well. By this point, they are having a ball. They feel like partners. They are basking in their commonalities, and at the same time open and eager to learn about their differences. They radiate an overall sense of trust and belonging.

For the last phase of this exercise, we pause them in this moment. We ask them what they are feeling. "Excited," "invigorated," or "renewed" are the responses we typically get, as they exchange affirming and knowing looks with people they just met. We explain that what they are feeling is the sense of belonging in the midst of differences. It's the power of inclusion. And then we ask, "What if you could produce these feelings outside this room—in your life, in your workspace? What if every day, like right now, you were intrinsically motivated to reach out to someone you don't know, and discover and discuss with curiosity the similarities and differences between you? What if your brain's automatically activated attitude were to rejoice in what makes us 'uniquely me and uniquely you'? What would that add to your work, to your knowledge base, to your life?"

There was a time when we thought that getting a majority of people to maintain such a mindset consistently was nearly impossible once they stepped outside that meeting room—when there are deadlines to be met and decision after decision to be made. But as we begin to help organizations implement the necessary education and fine-tune their environments informed by social neuroscience and social psychology, all with the goal of fostering intrinsic inclusion, we see real transformation. Most exciting, we are just at the beginning of this journey. We have so many more questions to ask, and so much more to learn about brain functioning and what it reveals for DEI.

8

AN INVITATION

When we are our best selves with each other,
I don't think that's what's possible between people,
I believe that's what's true between people.
And I don't think we have to work to make it true
between people. I think we just have to get the stuff
out of the way that's stopping it from happening.

—BRENE BROWN[53]

In an effort to help two nonprofit boards hammer out the details of a proposed merger (they were behaving more like the Hatfields and McCoys than future partners), we presented them with two questions:

- What does the future look like if you don't find a way to work together?
- What does it look like if you do?

Then, we handed them a mock newspaper sheet dated five years in the future. On one side, the headline reads, "Community Loses Services of [name of the smaller, less established partner]. Assets Auctioned. Outreach Center Closed." The other side's headline reads, "Nonprofit Surpasses All Expectations. Benefits to Community Grow Exponentially. Mission Expands."

The very hurdles our differences create—the ones that feel threatening at first—can become the sources of strength, resilience, and direction that allow us to realize our ambition even more fully than we thought possible. DEI is no longer about "working through" our differences. The future is in learning to "work with" our differences—and getting them to work for us.

Today, every organization needs to ask: "Where will we be in five years if we don't become more intrinsically inclusive? If we don't meaningfully diversify our leadership ranks? If we don't encourage an explorer's mindset throughout our organization?"

The organization will still exist, most likely, but it will be far less competitive.

Forty-seven percent of millennials (young adults in their twenties and thirties) see workplace diversity and inclusion as an important consideration in their job search.[54]

The International Monetary Fund (IMF) projected emerging markets and developing economies as responsible for nearly 60 percent of worldwide GDP in 2018 and climbing.[55] Those are the facts.

For a company to operate successfully in this global marketplace, it must have a visceral understanding of the people and cultures that make up those emerging economies—not just China, Mexico, and Brazil, but also Zambia, Costa Rica, Vietnam, Nigeria, Swaziland, and many others. That's where the middle class is growing and where new customers are to be found.

If your business hasn't developed leaders who are native to the regions and cultures you wish to serve, you aren't positioned to meet the needs of their people or businesses. And if your company's leadership isn't diversified, you aren't in a position to attract the best and the brightest to that leadership.

DEI Is On the Crest of a Wave

For all these realities, reasons, and more, we are more committed than ever to using the insights and direction gained from social neuroscience and social psychology in advancing diversity, equity, and inclusion. In just what we've already learned and put into practice, these sciences have placed DEI on the crest of a wave of breakthroughs.

As we have come to understand the origins, thought processes, and physiology around bias, implicit bias, stereotyping, and intrinsic motivation have fundamentally changed our approach from the external matters to working more with internal matters. Our education, systems, practices, and policies are now geared toward encouraging clients to open their own minds and increasing their awareness, all with the goal of becoming intrinsically inclusive.

This powerful and sustainable approach to DEI clearly resonates with clients. When people can understand their thought processes and can learn to catch and evaluate their automatically activated attitudes, it has a profound effect. Beyond issues of diversity, equity, and inclusion and business success, it enhances their lives.

Needless to say, neuroscience has energized our work. And we're already taking next steps to bring more neuroscience to DEI. We're currently working on partnerships with laboratories and researchers in both the United States and Europe. As the scientists help us to stay abreast of the latest discoveries in neuroscience and findings in social psychology, our team will be actively looking at ways to integrate what we learn into the workplace to advance DEI.

Some of our current questions include: "Can virtual reality allow colleagues to walk in each other's shoes? Can it allow us to experience ourselves with a different skin color, height, or age? And would these experiences create new levels of respectful empathy? Can it create events or frequent exposures significant enough to stop automatically activated attitudes?" And, of course, we want to track our work to see whether these science-inspired solutions result in significant increases in diversity in the workforce, particularly in the upper tiers of leadership.

To chronicle our journey and allow all who are interested in DEI to benefit from what we find, we've set up a website (www.intrinsicinclusion.com). On it, you'll find reports on the latest in neuroscience relating to DEI, new systems and practices we've employed, results from our field experiments, and any information that can help DEI to progress.

And now this is where you come in ....

JOIN THE DISCUSSION

We want you (our readers) to join us on this journey and become part of the conversation in finding out how exactly—in practical terms—we can reboot our brains against bias and toward inclusion. In addition to providing you with our findings, we want our website to become a community where everyone can share ideas, collect information, celebrate what works, and analyze what doesn't. We are inviting you right here and right now to post to our site:

- Any and all of your DEI triumphs and success stories. What has worked? Where have you experienced resistance? Where does your organization get stuck?

- Your thoughts on the information presented in this book—on neuroscience and DEI. What rings true? What doesn't? Which of the practices discussed here have interested you? Have you tried them?

- Any neuroscience-inspired strategy you've designed and put into practice in your organization. And the results, of course.

- Anything else dealing with neuroscience, social psychology, and DEI that you want to bring to the group's attention or explore with others.

Our hope is that through our work with scientists, our own practice, and what you, our readers, bring to the discussion, we'll be able to break down the barriers to DEI—especially the ones in our own heads—and give organizations the tools and strategies they need to reboot biased brains and achieve and enjoy the benefits of diversity and inclusion.

As we said at the beginning, this is a book of questions more than answers. We are on a new frontier in diversity, equity, and inclusion, one that has the potential to prove significant and transformative, not just for businesses but for society as a whole.

When we ask ourselves, "What will DEI look like five years from now if we continue to pursue this neuroscience-based approach?" we can honestly answer that it looks productive, promising, and very bright.

EPILOGUE

by BETH GIGLIO

Senior Vice President Human Resources, 84.51°

As you've seen, Janet and Vincent have opened a whole new avenue for the study of DEI, since Janet first posed that trailblazing question: "Is there a way to reboot our brains so we're naturally motivated to move toward those who aren't like us, instead of away from them?" It's an avenue with the potential to bring about groundbreaking advances in this field—including the opportunity to grow leaders and drive inclusive work environments by addressing the areas in our brain that actually create bias in the first place.

At 84.51°, we use data and science to help make customers' lives easier. Janet and Vincent use data and science to help understand what needs to be addressed to drive inclusion. They've helped us realize that to truly achieve our purpose of making customers' lives easier, our data and the lenses we use to understand the data need to be unbiased. Recognizing bias and raising awareness helps—but what Janet and Vincent are solving for is the root cause of bias. If we can address that, it is far more powerful than just "mitigating" risks for bias. Our love of data and science, diagnosing and recognizing patterns, and solving really difficult problems brought our teams together, and we are so proud to be the inaugural donor to this cutting-edge research.

The Intrinsic Inclusion Institute is led by Dr. Rezai and was founded in February 2019 as part of the West Virginia University Rockefeller Neuroscience Institute. Dr. Rezai will continue to provide guidance as Janet and Vincent recruit top researchers in neuroscience and continue to explore their work in intrinsic inclusiveness.

We invite you to join with us on this amazing journey! The Intrinsic Inclusion Institute will graciously accept monetary donations and more sponsors like 84.51°, and we also want to have highly engaged participants along the way. We want the Intrinsic Inclusion Institute to be an open platform, a true learning community; a working collaborative between business and science. We want you to follow the progress of the Intrinsic Inclusion Institute, and we want to follow yours as you put the concepts from this book to work. The goal is for us to help each other become more intrinsically inclusive, so together we can create a better world. To find out exactly how to get involved and learn more about the Intrinsic Inclusion Institute, visit www.intrinsicinclusion.com.

ACKNOWLEDGMENTS

On many levels, the ideas, practical applications, and newfound direction for DEI explored in this book are themselves products of diversity and inclusion. By bringing together people from very different worlds—corporate professionals with empirical knowledge gained over decades in the DEI field and a host of academic researchers responsible for the latest scientific findings on human interaction—we were able to see and discuss DEI in an entirely new light. This collaboration of diverse ideas, experiences, and approaches opened up a conversation that had been stuck for years, established new avenues for action, and produced a contagious, fresh energy for the possibilities of diversity, equity, and inclusion among everyone who participated.

As this book took shape at every stage—collecting, debating, understanding, and organizing the information, and then writing, rewriting, editing, and producing—we were blessed with corporate colleagues and mentors who championed the mission; academics, scientists, and professionals willing to lend their specific knowledge and talents to our effort; and, of course, our family and friends always willing to have a discussion, give another point of view, put up with our long hours, and sustain us with their love and their full support.

We'd especially like to recognize and thank Samuel Lynch, who as one of the founders of Global Lead helped chart this amazing path into diversity, equity, and inclusion with us all those many years ago. It has taken us to places we never could have anticipated. Sam has always been the uplifting spirit behind this work.

We are also eternally grateful to all the amazingly talented people of Global Lead, Global Novations, BRBS World, and V. Randolph Brown Consulting, and to our former partners Oris Stuart, John Peoples, Michel Hyter, and Martin Chavez. All embody and live diversity, equity, and inclusion.

A heartfelt thanks to each of our treasured clients. Without them, this work would not have been possible.

We give our unending admiration to Dr. David A. Thomas for his enlightening, pioneering, and inspiring work in diversity and inclusion. Through his efforts, our mission gained even more purpose and urgency.

And we thank Beth Brand for serving as our faithful guide and scribe along the journey to produce this book. Her spirit pervades these pages.

For their kindness and patience as we began and now continue our exploration into neuroscience and the power of intrinsic inclusion for business, we cannot even begin to express the extent of our appreciation for all the scientists—Dr. Russell Fazio, Dr. Steven Spencer, Dr. Dylan Wagner, Dr. Baldwin Way, Dr. Andrea Serino, Dr. John Campo, Dr. Bart Barthelemy, Dr. Scott Galster, and Dr. Chelsea Kane—who shared and explained their research to us or simply championed our endeavors. They opened our eyes to new possibilities in fostering dynamic human relationships. We look forward to further collaboration.

And, of course, we owe a huge debt of gratitude to Dr. Ali Rezai, who so enthusiastically contemplated our initial question, encouraged us, and then so generously worked with us to find the brightest minds to shine a new light on and open a whole new world to the field of diversity, equity, and inclusion.

JANET

I thank God for giving me a life mission to bring different people together in greater understanding and greater grace.

I also thank God for giving me my husband, Dr. Calvin Washington, whose love, support, patience, and humor have been the foundation upon which I rest. And I celebrate and appreciate the strength I receive from our very diverse and inclusive immediate family, Dr. Amanda Reid and our son-in-law, Daniel Freeman; Leon Reid, IV and our daughter-in-law, Caroline Reid; Veronica Washington; and Kyle Washington. And, of course, our grandchildren, Lillian and Alex Freeman and Holly Reid, who make the world a more welcoming place.

My deep gratitude goes out to my parents, Dr. Broadus and Lillian Butler; my grandmother, Mrs. Lillian Swan Rutherford; and my brother, Dr. Bruce N. Butler—all of whom raised me and gave me a foundation.

To my business partner and "brother by love" of more than thirty years, Vincent R. Brown, I give thanks for your creative genius. We have truly leveraged our differences and similarities to forge a relationship that has been immensely personally rewarding, as well as helpful and healing to so many others.

And a special acknowledgment to special friends—Walter and Stephanie White, Leonard and Lynn Small, Angela and

Leon Durham, Pamela and Lou Ramsey, LaToya Everett, and Patricia Melford—for their love and fun, and for making a "family by love."

VINCENT

First and foremost, I give thanks to the Almighty, who has blessed me beyond measure and put so many wonderful people in my path.

Then, I must express my thanks to Janet, the smartest person I know, for being a great business partner, friend, and sister.

And of course, I owe my entire family a debt of gratitude for everything they do and are: Valencia, who has been an amazing life partner and mother for so many years; Michael, Adam, and Steven, my three sons, who have served as my inspiration to make the world a little better; D'Ana, my daughter in love with Michael, who together have provided me the greatest gift and inspiration of all, my grandsons, Kayson and Kylan, Adam and Zoe with Cayden on the way; my dad and mom, Roosevelt and Arthenia, who are smiling from above; and my brother, Mark, who, like me, embodies their spirits.

I am also indebted to my family in love, Joey and Alicia, and my niece, Amya, for their unconditional support.

I am deeply grateful for Pamela Ramsey, LaToya Everett, Angela Durham, Erik Zito, Alex Alvarez, and all other VRBC consultants and partners, who support and inspire me daily.

Finally, because, we share so many friends and family and loved ones, to all those acknowledged by Janet—ditto.

AND HERE'S TO YOU

Last but so very far from least, we thank you, our reader, for investing your time in learning more about diversity and inclusion. As the world becomes smaller, the issue of diversity, equity, and inclusion will only get larger. And people like you who choose to stay curious and informed about the latest DEI developments will be uniquely positioned to make our world a better place. So, thank you. And we hope to see you taking part in, and adding to, the discussions on our website: www.intrinsicinclusion.com. Please join us.

ABOUT THE AUTHORS

JANET B. REID, PH.D.

As President/CEO of BRBS World, LLC, Janet leads a group that serves forward-leaning clients whose growth depends on building world-class leaders. Her extensive experience designing, researching, and leading highly effective diversity, equity, and inclusion initiatives began at Procter & Gamble. She continues this work across the globe by developing measurable strategies, keynote speaking, facilitating, coaching, and advising.

VINCENT R. BROWN

Vincent is President/CEO of V. Randolph Brown Consulting, providing facilitated learning experiences that help teams create and sustain change in multiple fields and practice areas including healthcare, financial services, retail, and professional services. Central to his innovative work in diversity, equity, and inclusion is his thought leadership on cognitive diversity.

Brown and Reid co-founded the international consulting firm Global Novations, a former Goldman Sachs portfolio company. *Intrinsic Inclusion: Rebooting Your Biased Brain* is their third book.

ENDNOTES

CHAPTER 1

1   Dan Ariely, "Transcript of 'Are We in Control of Our Own Decisions?'" *TED: Ideas Worth Spreading*, December 2008, www.ted.com/talks/ dan_ariely_asks_are_we_in_control_of_our_own_decisions/ transcript?utm_campaign=BeepBeepBites%2B-%2BNieuwsbrief.

2   Josh Bersin, "Why Diversity and Inclusion Will Be A Top Priority for 2016," *Forbes* (December 6, 2015), https://www.forbes.com/sites/ joshbersin/2015/12/06/why-diversity-and-inclusion-will-be-a- top-priority-for-2016.

3   Association of Governing Boards of Universities and Colleges, Top Strategic Issues for Boards 2016–2017 (2016): 24–26.

4   Grace Donnelly and Stacey Jones, "The White House Tech Inclusion Pledge, A Year Later," *Fortune* (June 2, 2017), http://fortune.com/2017/06/22/ tech-diversity-white-house-pledge-year-later, updated July 24, 2017.

5   CIA, *Director's Diversity In Leadership Study: Overcoming Barriers to Advancement* (2014), https://www.cia.gov/library/reports/dls-report.pdf.

CHAPTER 2

6   Walt Kelly, *Pogo: We Have Met the Enemy and He Is Us* (New York: Simon & Schuster, 1972).

7   Russell H. Fazio, "Understanding Implicit Bias: Automatically-Activated Attitudes, Motivation, and Opportunity," presented at the Neuroscience of Diversity and Inclusion Workshop, Columbus, OH, 2016.

8   Mike Cardwell, *Dictionary of Psychology* (1996).

9   Marianne Bertrand and Sendhil Mullainathan, "Are Emily and Greg More Employable Than Lakisha and Jamal? A Field Experiment on Labor Market Discrimination," *American Economic Review* (September 2004), http://www.uh.edu/~adkugler/Bertrand&Mullainathan.pdf.

10 Russell H. Fazio, "Understanding Implicit Bias: Automatically-Activated Attitudes, Motivation, and Opportunity," presented at the Neuroscience of Diversity and Inclusion Workshop, Columbus, OH, 2016.

11 Ibid.

12 Baldwin Way, from interview conducted by the author in September 2016.

13 Jason P. Mitchell, C. Neil Macrae, and Mahzarin R. Banaji. "Dissociable medial prefrontal contributions to judgments of similar and dissimilar others," *Neuron* (May 2006).

14 Thomas F. Pettigrew, "The Ultimate Attribution Error: Extending Allport's Cognitive Analysis of Prejudice," *Personality and Social Psychology Bulletin* 5, no. 4 (1979): 461–76.

15 Massey, Douglas S., *Categorically Unequal: The American Stratification System* (Russell Sage Foundation, 2007).

16 Stephen Bloom, "Lessons of a Lifetime," *Smithsonian* (September 2005), https://www.smithsonianmag.com/science-nature/lesson-of-a-lifetime-72754306.

17 Steven Spencer, *Four Prejudice Paradigms that Interface with Neuroscience,* presented at the Neuroscience of Diversity and Inclusion Workshop, Columbus, OH, 2016.

18 Elizabeth J. Carter and Kevin A. Pelphrey, "Friend or Foe? Brain Systems Involved in the Perception of Dynamic Signals of Menacing and Friendly Social Approaches," *Social Neuroscience* (2008).

19 Edward R. Murrow, "A Visit to Flat Rock: Carl Sandburg," *See It Now,* 1954, CBS News, Season 4, Episode 6.

CHAPTER 3

20 David A. Thomas, "Diversity as Strategy," *Harvard Business Review* (September 2004), https://hbr.org/2004/09/diversity-as-strategy.

21 Benedict Carey, "Chip, Implanted in Brain, Helps Paralyzed Man Regain Control of Hand," *New York Times* (April 4, 2016).

CHAPTER 4

22 Public Broadcasting Service, *Makers: Women Who Make America,* Gloria Steinem interview, 2013.

23 Carlos D. Navarette, Daniel M.T. Fessler, and Serena J. Eng, "Elevated Ethnocentrism in the First Trimester of Pregnancy," *Evolution and Human Behavior* 28 (2007): 60–65.

24 Muzafer Sherif et al., "Intergroup Conflict and Cooperation: The Robbers Cave Experiment," (1954, 1961), https://psychclassics.yorku.ca/Sherif/chap1.htm. An internet resource developed by Christopher D. Green, York University, Toronto, Ontario.

25 Russell H. Fazio, from an interview with the authors, August 2016.

26 Steven J. Spencer, *Four Prejudice Paradigms that Interface with Neuroscience*, presented at the Neuroscience of Diversity and Inclusion Workshop, Columbus, OH, 2016.

27 W.E.B. Du Bois, *The Souls of Black Folk* (New York: Dover Publications, 1941).

28 Steven J. Spencer, Claude M. Steele, and Diane M. Quinn. "Stereotype Threat and Women's Math Performance," *Journal of Experimental Social Psychology* (1999).

29 Steven J. Spencer, *Four Prejudice Paradigms that Interface with Neuroscience*, presented at the Neuroscience of Diversity and Inclusion Workshop, Columbus, OH, 2016.

30 Jim Blascovich et al., "African Americans and High Blood Pressure: The Role of Stereotype Threat," *Psychological Science* (May 2001).

31 Toni Schmader and Michael Johns, "Converging Evidence that Stereotype Threat Reduces Working Memory Capacity," *Journal of Personality and Social Psychology* (September 2003): 440–52.

32 Sinthujaa Sampasivam et al., "The Effects of Outgroup Threat and Opportunity to Derogate on Salivary Cortisol Levels," *International Journal Environmental Research and Public Health* (June 2016).

33 July Y. Huang, Joshua M. Ackerman, and John A. Bargh, "Superman to the Rescue: Stimulating Physical Involuntary Attenuates Exclusion-Related Interpersonal Biases," *Journal of Experimental Social Psychology* (May 1, 2013): 349–54.

34 Claudia Goldin and Cecelia Rouse, "Orchestrating Impartiality: The Impact of 'Blind' Auditions on Female Musicians," *American Economic Review* 90, no. 4 (2000): 715–41.

CHAPTER 5

35   Edward L. Deci and Richard M. Ryan, "Self-Determination Theory and the Facilitation of Intrinsic Motivation, Social Development, and Well-Being," *American Psychologist* (January 2000): 72.

36   Ibid., 69.

37   Ibid., 70.

38   Ibid., 69.

39   Ibid., 68.

40   Ibid., 70.

CHAPTER 6

41   Russell H. Fazio and Michael A. Olson, "The MODE Model: Attitude-Behavior Processes as a Function of Motivation and Opportunity," in Dual Process Theories of the Social Mind, ed. J.W. Sherman, B. Gawronski, and Y. Trope (New York: Guilford Press, 2014), http://faculty.psy.ohiostate.edu/fazio/fazio/documents/FazioOlson_DualProcessVolume__Feb062013.pdf.

42   Ibid.

43   Jean-Paul Noel, Christian Pfeiffer, Olaf Bianke and Andrea Serino, "Peri-personal Space as the Space of Bodily Self," *Cognition.* 2015 Nov.; 144: 49–57.

44   Jean-Paul Noel et al., "I Feel What You Feel If I Like You: the Effect of Attractiveness on Visual Remapping of Touch," *Multisensory Research 27* (Koninklijke Brill NV, Leiden, 2014): 43–54.

45   Russell H. Fazio, "Understanding Implicit Bias: Automatically Activated Attitudes, Motivation, and Opportunity," presented at the Neuroscience of Diversity and Inclusion Workshop. Columbus, OH, 2016.

46   Ibid.

CHAPTER 7

47   Scott E. Page, *The Difference: How the Power of Diversity Creates Better Groups, Firms, Schools, and Societies* (Princeton University Press, 2007).

48   Project Implicit, Frequently Asked Questions, https://implicit.harvard.edu/implicit/faqs.html.

49 Russell H. Fazio, interview with the author, August 2016.

50 Gregory M. Walton, Steven J. Spencer, and Sam Erman, "Affirmative Meritocracy," *Social Issues and Policy Review* 7, no. 1 (2013): 1–35.

51 Steven J. Spencer, interview with the author, August 2016.

52 Ibid.

CHAPTER 8

53 Brené Brown, "Strong Back, Soft Front, Wild Heart," *The On Being Project*, February 2018, onbeing.org/programs/brene-brown-strong-back-soft-front-wild-heart-feb2018.

54 Sarab Kochhar, "Nearly Half of American Millennials Say a Diverse and Inclusive Workplace Is an Important Factor in a Job Search," The Institute for Public Relations, 2016, https://instituteforpr.org/nearly-half-american-millennials-say-diverse-inclusive-workplace-important-factor-job-search.

55 International Monetary Fund, "GDP based on PPP, share of world," (October 2017), www.imf.org/external/datamapper/PPPSH@WEO/OEMDC/ADVEC/WEOWORLD.